WARTIME EASTBOURNE

The story of the most raided town in the south-east

GEORGE HUMPHREY

The Author

George Humphrey was born in Eastbourne on New Year's Eve, 1922, attended Christ Church and Willowfield Central Schools and, in April 1937, joined T.R. Beckett Ltd (owners of the Eastbourne Gazette and Herald) as an apprentice compositor. In 1938 he joined the Air Defence Cadet Corps (forerunner of the ATC) and in May 1940 left to join the LDV/Home Guard in which he served — reaching the rank of Platoon Sergeant — until entering the RAF in September 1942 to serve as an armourer. He returned to T.R. Beckett as a proof-reader in January 1947 and began his researches into Eastbourne at war. He took early retirement in 1986. He has had nineteen novels published.

Published by BECKETT FEATURES
T.R. Beckett Ltd
1 Commercial Road, Eastbourne BN21 3XQ.
Telephone: Eastbourne (0323) 22091

First published 1989
Copyright © Beckett Features 1989

ISBN 1 871986 00 1

Design by Beckett Features, origination by TRB Typesetting/TRB Graphics. Printed and bound by Anchor Press Ltd, Tiptree, Essex.

Contents

A town that survived

FOR MORE THAN four years during the Second World War, Eastbourne was in the front line. Not solely because of its location on the Channel coast facing a France already occupied by Germany but because it was chosen by the enemy as a target for heavy aerial bombardment.

Eastbourne, then a totally self-governing County Borough and high class holiday resort, provided no obvious reason for this assault and the air raids were frequently referred to as 'terror attacks' as all too often the bombs struck buildings which could have no possible military importance. But, for just a few weeks in 1940 and on one or two isolated occasions during the years which followed, the Luftwaffe did have some military justification for their persistent pounding of the town.

After the fall of France in 1940, Hitler, holding the French Channel ports, began contemplating an invasion of Britain — at first half-heartedly but soon with real intent. The invasion plan, 'Operation Sea Lion', was modified so many times that the final plan is often lost among the innumerable earlier schemes. The fact, however, remains that Eastbourne was suddenly seen as an important communications centre in the coastal defence system and the Germans felt it should be 'softened-up' so that the leading elements of their 26th Infantry Division landing at Pevensey Bay and their 6th Mountain Division, due to attack at Cuckmere Haven, should not be harassed by defenders centred on Eastbourne.

On this basis Eastbourne was, for a few weeks, a legitimate target. Following the indefinite postponement of the invasion, however, the town had little or nothing to commend it as a military target and

This 500kg bomb dropped on Friday, June 4, 1943, passed through St Saviour's Vicarage and into the church without exploding. It was later defused.

thereafter the air raids became terror raids in the strictest sense. In fact, the few legitimate targets in the town appear to have suffered least though, of these, the railway station and tracks, and the gasworks certainly took some punishment.

Eastbourne's war may be divided into phases. Following the time of the 'Phoney War' from September 3, 1939, to April 1940, came the first serious period extending over some twelve months spanning parts of 1940 and 1941, when air raids were made chiefly by medium bombers. These aircraft mostly comprised the ubiquitous Dornier Do17 'Flying Pencil', although Junkers Ju88s

The shattered remains of Barclays Bank, Terminus Road, bombed on March 7, 1943.

were also seen and Heinkel He111s occasionally bombed by night.

At first many of the Dorniers carried the bomb loads they had employed in support of the troops in France — as many as fifteen or sixteen small high explosive bombs mostly of about 50kg — or, alternatively, three 250kg high explosive bombs and one 50kg oil incendiary bomb. Often 'sticks' (lines of bombs falling in succession) would overlap and lead to some confusion as to where one stick ended and the other began, whereas 'salvos'

Eastbourne railway station took its fair share of knocks. A fighter-bomber dropped the bomb which tore up tracks between platforms 2 and 3 on March 14, 1943.

(bombs bunched together) were generally more easily defined.

These attacks came to an end during 1941 but were followed in 1942 by the ferocious assaults by groups of fighter-bombers which came in at rooftop height across the town, raking the streets, houses and buses with cannon and machinegun fire before releasing their bombs. Each plane carried one or two larger-capacity high explosive bombs of 250kg or 500kg calibre — far more potent weapons than those of similar size employed earlier. The town suffered severely from these attacks which occurred at intervals for more than a year.

The fighter-bombers ended their assault in the summer of 1943 and subsequently there were more night attacks, some on residential areas, some on open ground at the outskirts of the town.

There followed a few months' respite and then, in June 1944, began the menace of the Flying Bombs — the V1. These were intended for London but, launched from various sites along the French coast, they came across the south coast of England day after day and, when the London anti-aircraft defences were moved down to the coast, the V1s were met with a massive concentration of accurate fire. Some fell to attacking fighter planes and some were even turned back to France when the fighter pilots tipped the wings of the V1s until they faced the wrong way.

The magnitude of Eastbourne's ordeal may be gauged by the fact that after the war it was officially declared that the town received more attacks than any other in the south-eastern region — as evidenced by some of the statistics here briefly outlined.

There were 112 air raids involving actual bombing; 671 high explosive bombs of up to 1,000kg calibre; 90 unexploded bombs; 28 oil incendiaries of 50kg calibre; 4,000 Thermite incendiaries of 2kg calibre. There were 1,106 civilian casualties — 174 fatal, 443 seriously injured, 489 slightly hurt. A total of 475 houses were totally destroyed,

The wreckage of 38 Whitley Road, one victim of the first bombing raid on Eastbourne, Sunday, July 7, 1940.

7

1,000 seriously damaged and 10,000 slightly damaged.

Sirens sounded 1,350 general alerts which often came too late to be of any use and, when they were finally introduced, there were 861 local warnings.

The final toll was heavy enough but how much worse it would have been but for the compulsory and recommended evacuations of large numbers of children and non-essential adults in the early summer and again in the autumn of 1940. It has been claimed that the population — generally estimated to have been 60,000 in 1939 — was reduced to a mere 13,000 at one point.

A quite remarkable spirit of comradeship and fortitude was displayed by those who remained to cope with the air attacks and those who, if the worst should happen, were ready to meet the expected invasion.

Before the war, the Government had laid down rules for issuing air raid warnings. All reports of approaching aircraft must go to a Regional Controller who, in Eastbourne's case, was some thirty miles away to the north, in Kent; only the Regional Controller could then decide if the aircraft posed a threat and order the sounding of a general alert on the sirens which covered an extremely wide area of the south-east. No sirens were to be sounded for single raiders.

This ruling led to the town being bombed without prior warning far too often or, in some cases, being bombed while the general all-clear was sounding. Eventually, and only after tremendous pressure was applied to the Home Office, a local warning system was arranged — the sound, instead of issuing as a rising and falling double off-key wail from a double-banked siren, was modified to issue each note separately and alternately, thus producing a peculiar cuckoo-like sound — hence the local name 'cuckoo warning'.

Some of the constant tension was lifted by this improvement but, despite the strain of raids endured and raids threatened, the life of the town went on as normally as possible.

Risks became a part of life and were accepted stoically in order to rescue trapped persons and this was recognised by the award of two MBEs, four George Medals and a number of commendations. The award most welcomed by the people of the town, however, was that of the Girl Guides' Gilt Cross given posthumously to seventeen-year-old Peggy Harland — of which more later.

Towards the end of this book will be given a list of credits for all those who led the various essential services in the town during its years of trial but there are six men who should be mentioned here.

Councillor (later Alderman) Arthur Edward Rush was the Mayor of Eastbourne through the worst of the ordeal. He and Mr Francis H. Busby, the Town Clerk, were ever-present whenever bombs fell in the town, helping, consoling, arranging assistance and comfort — and both earned the respect and gratitude of all who remained in the town.

The other four deserving of our gratitude as well as that of people of

A V1 Flying Bomb was shot down behind Astaire Avenue on July 4, 1944 and caused tremendous blast damage to houses which subsequently had to be demolished.

their own time, are the photographers: Wilfred Bignell of T.R. Beckett Ltd, proprietors of the Eastbourne Gazette and Herald; Harry C. Deal, who supplied pictures for the Eastbourne Chronicle and Eastbourne Courier; Roy Hudson, freelance photographer; and John Wills. Without the efforts of these men, the pictures which make up the bulk of this publication would never have been available.

NOTE: Throughout this volume it will be seen that the various parts of the town and particular structures are given their correct names, not the misnomers of today. Street names and numbers, business names and so on are given as they were during the war. The term 'civilian' is properly applied to public, police, fire brigade and all the other civilian organisations. The term 'Civil Defence' is rarely used, 'ARP' being preferred. The word 'mission' in reference to air attacks is avoided since it was never used during the war by any British service — 'operation' or 'sortie' were the British terms. The word 'mission' arrived in Britain with the Americans and was applied by themselves to their own activities.

Firemen demonstrate hose drill at the Wish Tower, 1939.

A Petty-Officer, 'Tiffies' and 'Matelots' celebrate VE Day with music at the junction of South Street and Gildredge Road.

Above: The rarely-recognised Women's Transport Service pose for a group picture. *Right*: The first volunteers for the Women's Voluntary Service on parade, 1939. *Below*: Nurses of a Red Cross Voluntary Aid Detachment on parade, 1939. *Bottom of the page*: Members of the Air Defence Cadet Corps (forerunner of the Air Training Corps) provide 'casualties' for the ARP exercise in 1939.

Overture and beginners

WARS RARELY OCCUR without some prior warning signs and even when they seem to catch authority with its guard down, there is usually someone, somewhere who has foreseen the impending disaster and begun to take the appropriate precautions. After the murderous losses incurred in the First World War, the British were very much opposed to war and would have moved heaven and earth to avoid another but they failed to take into account the rising tide of German national pride.

Winston Churchill, so often branded a 'warmonger' by those who never truly study the facts, was one such man. For several years he warned of German re-armament and growing militarism but he was crying in the wilderness and little or nothing was done to prevent or, at worst, prepare for the inevitable conflict.

However, among the things which were done, was the provision of anti-gas respirators for the whole populace — even down to babes in arms — for poison gas was then seen in much the same light as are nuclear weapons today. Also prepared were booklets of instructions on how to create a gas-proof and blast-proof room for every household and a new organisation was set up to control air raid precautions. It is generally considered that this widespread provision of respirators and knowledge of how to cope with poison gas was largely responsible for the notable absence of war gases during the conflict.

In September 1938, Prime Minister Neville Chamberlain went to Munich to try to secure peace with Hitler but only succeeded in negotiating away Czechoslovakia. His claim that he had negotiated 'peace in our time' was happily accepted by many, sadly doubted by the majority and openly ridiculed by others. Not that anyone wanted or looked forward to a war — it was just painfully obvious that barring a miracle it could not be long before we were in fact at war.

During the ensuing twelve months strenuous efforts were made to re-equip and mechanise the Army, update the Royal Air Force and prepare the Navy for war. Air raid wardens were recruited all over the country, as were first aid parties, auxiliary firemen, gas decontamination squads, rescue squads, war reserve policemen, voluntary nurses and many other much-needed services.

In January 1939, Eastbourne was officially designated a 'safety zone' and warned to expect London evacuees in the event of war.

Three months later, Eastbourne's MP, Mr Charles Taylor, was reported to have told a meeting of the Junior Imperial League that he did not think Eastbourne need worry about being bombed in time of war ...the attackers, whoever they might be, would not go to the trouble of carrying high explosive bombs for the purpose of bombing Eastbourne.

In April a leading London evening paper said it believed Eastbourne's ARP scheme was further advanced than that of any other town in the country. And, in May, the Regional

Two girls 'model' the robust 'civilian duty' respirators in Terminus Road during an exercise in 1939.

The Mayor, Councillor Arthur Rush (centre), with in uniform, Chief Officer S.A. Phillips, of Eastbourne Fire Brigade, and Mr W.H. Smith, Chief Constable of Eastbourne, inspect a fire crew in 1939.

Commissioner (of ARP) suggested consideration of 'emergency arrangements necessary in the event of any district being bombed with consequent panic and the people rushing into open spaces and unable to return to their own homes...' He was an Englishman but he didn't really understand the English.

The situation deteriorated thereafter until, on August 23, 1939, the Home Office ordered the Chief Constable of Eastbourne to put air raid warnings into force. On September 1, the Luftwaffe bombed Warsaw and, to all intents and purposes, Britain was at war although it was not yet official. The blackout became operative and evacuation from London commenced on this day; 17,000 children and hospital patients began arriving at Eastbourne railway station in an unending succession of trains.

For three days the station was the scene of the ordered movement of thousands of people to buses, cars and ambulances for transport to billeting centres and thence to private homes or to hospitals.

Sunday, September 3, 1939. At 10am Chamberlain sent Hitler an ultimatum to end his attacks on Poland by 11am or face a declaration of war by Britain. This Hitler failed to do and Chamberlain's infinitely sad voice duly announced: '...therefore a state of war exists

An air raid warden looks on as two women wear civilian respirators and a baby is cocooned in an infant respirator which was hand-pumped by the mother.

between Germany and this country.' With the station crowded with evacuees awaiting transport and relays of trains moving in and out, the air raid sirens sounded but, thankfully, it was a false alarm.

From that time until March 20, 1940, Eastbourne, like most other British towns, found the blackout of houses and darkened streets a nuisance and the war itself little more than an inconvenient bore. The

13

London evacuee children arrive at Eastbourne railway station, September 1-3, 1939.

Eastbourne's lifeboat, the Jane Holland, alongside the stricken SS Barnhill — bombed on March 20, 1940. Twenty-nine crew were rescued while a tug and local firemen fought the blaze.

younger men had, of course, begun to leave to join the forces — those who had not already gone as Reservists or Territorials, that is — but their numbers were more than made up for by the evacuees.

The result was that there grew up a tendency for people to ascribe importance to the little irritations and restrictions. Worst of the bickering arose over the evacuees — the more stuffy townspeople claimed their 'guests' were foul-mouthed, ill-disciplined and dirty; the evacuees complained that they were poorly treated, ignored, or generally put upon. It was an argument no-one could win.

If there was anything worthwhile to emerge from the 'Phoney War', as one American journalist described the period of military stagnation, it was that people became accustomed to moving about in the dark and this was to stand them in good stead when the going got tough later in the year.

With the benefit of hindsight, it must seem incredible that 'muggings' were almost non-existent (the word certainly was), despite the apparently perfect conditions pre-

vailing every night of the year.

Vehicles were fitted with hoods for their headlights in the fond belief that enemy aircrews would not then be able to use them as a target marker. The result of this ploy was to make night driving a misery of eyestrain trying to spot the pedestrians who were almost invisible until they were within a few feet of the radiator. Fortunately, more and more cars were being laid-up for the duration because of petrol shortages and the chances of an accident were greatly reduced.

The horrors of war came home to many Eastbournians on Wednesday, March 20, 1940, when the SS Barnhill, a 5,000-ton merchant ship, was bombed and set ablaze in the Channel off Beachy Head between 10.30 and 11pm. Eastbourne's lifeboat, the Jane Holland (Coxswain Mike Hardy), attended, as did a tug from Newhaven. Four crewmen died in the explosion, another died in hospital soon after admission and seven other men were taken to hospital, among them the ship's captain, Michael O'Neill.

The latter had not been found at first but, after someone reported

The SS Barnhill, beached east of Langney Point, after the Eastbourne lifeboat took off the crew. Much freight was salvaged by local people.

hearing the ship's bell being rung, the ship was again boarded by Alec Huggett and Tom Allchorn from the Jane Holland. The risk these two men took was considerable as the vessel was blazing fiercely and the deck plates were almost red hot, but they found Captain O'Neill and

Eastbourne firemen fight the blaze aboard the SS Barnhill: March 20, 1940.

brought him to the lifeboat.

It transpired that Captain O'Neill, who suffered a fractured arm, a fractured collarbone and five broken ribs, had managed to crawl and roll some distance along the hot deck to ring the bell by pulling the rope with his teeth.

Local firemen were put aboard the ship with trailer pumps to fight the blaze and were still aboard three days later after the vessel had been beached just east of Langney Point. On that day the ship broke in two, after which five firemen were taken off by a fire float.

During ensuing weeks, the cargo of the Barnhill began to wash from the ruptured holds into the sea and thence to the beach where hundreds of people flocked to salvage tins of meat, stew, beans and so on. Officially everything was to be handed over to the responsible authority but little ever was.

The fearful sight of that vessel blazing out at sea, silhouetted against the clouds in the dawn light brought the war and all its horrors a great deal closer but even that was merely a harbinger of worse yet to come.

The curtain goes up

IN APRIL 1940, the Germans invaded and conquered Denmark and Norway following this with their assault on the Low Countries and France. The result of this 'Blitz-krieg' we all now know but the effect on a holiday town like Eastbourne, now only sixty-odd miles from the nearest German troops, was far-reaching and far less well recog-nised.

The Eastbourne lifeboat, the Jane Holland, and several local fishing and pleasure craft were sent to Dunkirk or St Valery to assist with the evacuation of the British Expeditionary Force. Some were lost. Some, like the Jane Holland, came home with severe but honourable battle scars.

The emotive word 'inva-sion', linked with the equally emotive 'paratroopers', became common in everyday conversation and it was generally considered that an in-vasion was not only likely but imminent, with enemy parachute troops leading the assault in massive numbers. The fact was that the German army was already over-stretched mopping-up in France and had no time to spare for such ventures. Nevertheless, the Govern-ment, now led by Winston Churchill, decided to call on ex-soldiers to form a force to be called the Local

Eastbourne's lifeboat was among several local boats that survived the evacuation of troops from Dunkirk and St Valery.

17

They're leaving home...

In July 1940 Eastbourne schoolchildren were evacuated to Hertfordshire and Bedfordshire to remove them from the invasion threat. Joining parents at the railway station was the Mayor, Councillor Arthur Rush (above).

Defence Volunteers to 'observe, report and harass' the enemy should he come. This force, better armed, equipped and trained than the popular image, was later re-named the Home Guard.

Defence works were commenced, with many local building firms working as Government sub-contractors. Pill-boxes (now mis-named 'bunkers'), anti-tank blocks (colloquially 'dragons' teeth') and traps were erected at many strategic points and along the beaches. The names of towns and villages were erased from road signs and from vehicles and hoardings. In June it became apparent that the Germans were at last making the first plans to assemble an invasion force to be thrown against England and in July the military imposed a seafront curfew in Eastbourne.

Also in July Eastbourne was

Birchfield's Stores was hit when a Dornier Do17 bombed Whitley Road on Sunday, July 7, 1940. This was the town's first taste of war.

Another scene of damage in Whitley Road — a foretaste of the destruction to follow.

The wreckage of a Messerschmitt Me110 twin-engined fighter, shot down over Meads on August 16, 1940. The plane crashed in the grounds of Aldro School and the dead pilot fell onto the roof of nearby Hill Brow School roof — the rear gunner drowned when he parachuted into the sea. Many people wrongly supposed this wreckage was that of a Heinkel He111 bomber.

proclaimed part of a defence area with restrictions on people entering a twenty-mile wide coastal belt; 3,000 local children followed the London evacuees from the town and ended up in Bedfordshire and Hertfordshire.

Sunday, July 7, 1940, 11.04am. A Dornier Do17, having passed over the radar station at Wartling and been turned away by anti-aircraft fire, swung round towards Eastbourne, crossed the Upperton district, lined-up on the axis of Whitley Road and released a stick of ten assorted high explosive bombs which fell between the junction with St Philip's Avenue and the junction with Avondale Road.

Mr Robert Woolliams, aged sixty, was killed and Mr William Turner died in hospital on the following Wednesday. Twenty-two people were injured, nine houses were destroyed and sixty damaged. Two large gas mains in the road were fractured. No warning had been given because of the national instruction that sirens should not be sounded for single raiders. The war had arrived in Eastbourne.

On August 16, the day on which the Battle of Britain really got under way as Hermann Goering gave the Luftwaffe specific orders to destroy the RAF before the invasion was launched, a running air battle swept down from the vicinity of RAF Kenley. Enemy aircraft were running for home, keeping low and jettisoning their bombs as they were pursued by RAF fighters.

A pandemonium of sound — aero-engines at full throttle, bombs, machine-guns, cannon. Suddenly there came an unworldly scream reaching a fearful crescendo and hardly a person in the town did not believe that here was a bomb with his or her name on it. Then silence — relatively speaking.

The noise had been made by the disintegrating wreckage of a Messerschmitt Me110 twin-engined fighter which fell in the grounds of Aldro School, Meads. The pilot's body was recovered from the roof of the nearby Hill Brow School and the gunner drowned when he parachuted into the sea. For years official records claimed the wreckage was that of a Heinkel He111 — despite the crew of only two — but, some time after the war, the pilot's widow,

Regulars of Eastbourne Fire Brigade, still wearing pre-war helmets, play a hose on a blazing gas main in Whitley Road: July 7, 1940. Eastbourne Gas Company men soon dealt with the leak.

Frau Hollekamp, visited the town and she proved that her husband (Hauptmann Ernst Hollekamp) had flown a Me110. A second raider was shot down into the sea off Beachy Head.

Records of the bombs dropped on the town are lost and information is sketchy but there were twenty-six, mostly in the Hampden Park area, such as Freeman Avenue, Brodrick Road and Rosebery Avenue. No houses were directly hit but there was considerable blast damage.

Corporation workmen Mr Frank Edwards, Mr Harry White and Mr Samuel Henman were collecting scrap for 'Salvage Week' and dived for cover beneath their lorry but a bomb exploded nearby in the road and splinters set the lorry ablaze. The two former died almost at once and the latter died in hospital.

Two young telephonists at the Hampden Park exchange — Miss M.L. May, aged nineteen, and Miss M.D. Sewell, aged seventeen — were commended for sticking to their post throughout the attack and handling vital calls from the ARP people.

This attack had the effect of prompting a 'Spitfire Fund' sponsored by T.R. Beckett Ltd, proprietors of the Eastbourne Gazette and Herald, with the

Recovering the body of the Me110's pilot from the roof of Hill Brow School. He was already dead when blown from his aircraft; the partial deployment of his parachute was coincidental.

The first raid on Eastbourne led to the setting up of a 'Spitfire Fund' by the publishers of the Eastbourne Gazette and Herald — which raised £1,000 more than its £5,000 target in just ten days. Here, the newspapers' counter clerk, Mabel Milton, poses with the collecting boxes.

intention of buying a Spitfire to bear the name of Eastbourne. This required subscriptions amounting to £5,000 — a princely sum in those days — and the people of the town responded by giving £6,000 in ten days. The whole cost of the collection was met by T.R. Beckett Ltd so that all the money gathered could be directed to the main purpose.

Daily, there was aerial activity of one kind or another as the Battle of Britain provided the most amazing spectacle. There were five minor night raids on the borough during the remainder of August but damage was generally slight. Then, at 5.15pm on August 31, there was a tremendous bang in Wish Road where two women were injured and some property was damaged. An intelligence officer of the Devonshire Regiment visited the scene and discovered fragments of an artillery shell of about four-inch calibre. The shell was later known to

have been fired from a U-boat which surfaced briefly before diving and moving on to Cuckmere Haven where it fired two more shells at Exceat Bridge. The shell-fire was merely a blind to conceal the U-boat's real purpose — taking pictures of the coast for the briefing of invasion personnel. This fact only came to light after the war when captured papers revealed the truth.

On Tuesday, September 10, a proclamation was posted about the town advising all those without essential duties to take advantage of an opportunity to evacuate to a safe area. Rail travel warrants were on offer for those wishing to go and details of how to make arrangements were included. On Wednesday, September 11, people were already on their way, eventually reducing the population to around 13,000.

Scene One was over, the real drama was about to begin.

The faces of war: *above*, a shocked woman is helped after an air raid by grim-faced rescuers while, *right*, a child smiles for the camera in Freeman Avenue, Hampden Park, where a bomb crater in a back garden was given some patriotic treatment.
Below: An Army intelligence officer of the 9th Battalion Devonshire Regiment examines a home in Wish Road damaged after a U-Boat shelled the town on August 31, 1940.

Rescuers move out onto the debris after at least one bomb struck the junction of Gildredge Road and Hyde Road on Friday, September 13, 1940.

An Austin 7 Ruby saloon car seems to have survived quite remarkably despite the proximity of the bombs at the junction of Gildredge Road and Hyde Road on Friday, September 13, 1940. This extensive damage was originally credited to one bomb but it now seems likely that two bombs fell in close company, two more falling behind the houses to the right of the picture.

Friday the Thirteenth

FOR GENERATIONS THE magic date, Friday the Thirteenth, has fascinated the superstitious but, on that day in September 1940, began a grim weekend ordeal for the town.

It was 3.55 in the afternoon and the railway station was crowded with those taking advantage of the Government advice that non-essential people should leave. Unfortunately, there were a number of key people who decided that their services could be better employed elsewhere and the ensuing shortage of trained personnel led to considerable confusion in logging the timing of the actual attacks and the fall of bombs on that weekend. Official reports at the time, and journalists' summaries since, have failed to completely clarify events but what is given here may be taken as a pretty fair account.

The Friday attacks were believed to have been made by three aircraft, one dropping a stick of ten assorted smaller bombs between Cornfield

A small bomb tore the front out of this house in Old Orchard Road in September 1940.

Christ Church Junior School was hit by a 50kg oil incendiary bomb and gutted by the subsequent fire on Friday, September 13, 1940. For years this building was wrongly described as the neighbouring Christ Church Infants School.

Road and Old Orchard Road but conflicting reports also record at least three more bombs in this stick and might even suggest yet another aircraft.

At about the same time another Dornier Do17 dropped a salvo of three 250kg HE bombs and one 50kg oil bomb in the Redoubt Ward. The latter struck Christ Church Junior School in Redoubt Road, gutting it (for years this was wrongly confused with the Infants School next door). One HE bomb struck Seaside and ignited a gas main; one fell at

the edge of Seaside Recreation Ground where it failed to explode and was left buried until after the war when it was found and detonated in situ. The third fell in the centre of the Recreation Ground and dug a massive crater. Four more bombs from another raider fell in the sea off the Cavendish Hotel.

Even this record raises further questions in that it is just possible that two or even three aircraft bombed the town centre and their loads overlapped.

Casualty figures are misleading but may be put at three dead and thirty injured.

Saturday, September 14, 1940. During the morning a Dornier Do17 flew across the town on reconnaissance but was attacked by two Spitfires and shot down in the sea. Satisfaction at this event was short-lived, however, for at 1.20pm two Dornier Do17s dropped eight bombs near the town centre between College Road and the rear of the Head Post Office. Two bombs failed to explode. Very soon afterwards there was a second

The raid on Friday the Thirteenth blasted the junction of Gildredge Road and Hyde Road.

Above: A typical example of the damage caused by a direct hit by one of the smaller HE bombs on a house at the junction of Susans Road and Longstone Road and, *right*, the shattered remains of the gardener's cottage, Manor House Grounds: both Saturday, September 14, 1940.
Below: Another scene of the destruction at the Gildredge Road and Hyde Road junction after the bombing raid on September 13, 1940.

attack, often wrongly confused with the first, in which twenty-one bombs were dropped between the sea opposite the Burlington Hotel and Leaf Road (off Ashford Road).

The majority of these were the smaller 'Daisy-Cutters' (a First World War term re-applied to 50kg and 70kg bombs in the Second) but full records do not exist since the warden service had been weakened by evacuation. Reports from the police and public were duly recorded and retained in lieu of the usual type.

At about 2.30 there was another attack in which four bombs fell around The Goffs and Gildredge Park and three others were also reported in Gildredge Park.

Another attack occurred at about 3.15pm, although reports confuse the time considerably. Devonshire Park took five HE; four more fell in the Firle Road/Dudley Road area and one on the beach near the York House Hotel which suggests three more in the sea. Seven unexploded bombs (UXBs) are recorded in St Philip's Avenue, adjacent allotments and Lottbridge Drove (an

eighth exploded in 1942). A number of 2kg incendiary bombs falling in Meads and at the Archery caused no trouble.

The day closed with a raid by three Do17s on Beachy Head Radar Station.

Seven people died and fifty were injured during a day which still provides grim memories for those who witnessed it. Officialdom may have declared that there were only two raids that afternoon but all who survived recall an almost continuous afternoon of bombing. Only sheer good fortune and evacuation kept the casualties to such a low figure.

On the following day — now celebrated as 'Battle of Britain Day' — the Luftwaffe came again at 7.05pm and dropped some seventeen HE bombs, one oil bomb and a large number of 2kg incendiaries between the Redoubt (now mis-named 'Redoubt Fortress') and Astaire Avenue. No casualties were recorded.

There has been much discussion as to why the town should have taken

The late Harry Deal, who provided the pictures for the Eastbourne Chronicle and Eastbourne Courier and whose work is strongly represented in this publication, catches his contemporary, the late Wilf Bignell (centre), photographer to the Eastbourne Gazette and Herald, camera in hand, studying blast damage in Longstone Road on September 14, 1940. In the foreground, War Reserve Constables gather household belongings for collection by their owners.

The rear wall was torn out of 85 Latimer Road when a bomb exploded in the back garden on Sunday evening, September 15, 1940.

such a battering on that weekend, only to be ignored for the next week, but the truth is that the town was being softened-up for the projected invasion. On Saturday, September 7, German shipping had moved westward into the Channel and a false-alarm of invasion had been issued but on the 15th/16th a similar movement drew sharp responses from the RAF, giving rise to many of the rumours of an invasion defeated at sea. The result was that on the 17th, the Germans decided at a staff conference that an invasion was not viable until the spring of 1941 and 'Operation Sea Lion' was postponed indefinitely, never again to receive serious consideration.

Hitler and company did not, however, deem it wise to inform the British of their decision and defence preparations continued. But the danger from seaborne and/or airborne assault was not over — the Royal Navy stated quite categorically that it could not guarantee to be able to intercept a 'raid in force' of up to 10,000 men before it could be landed.

Beltring Cottages, in Firle Road, were struck by a 250kg bomb during a raid in 1940.

On Sunday, September 22, 1940, at 5.15pm began a series of raids having no purpose in any invasion plans. Four HE bombs fell in the vicinity of Queen's Crescent, with one UXB falling in allotments on the north side of Seaside, remaining undiscovered until redevelopment began many years later. Four more landed near Whitley Road bridge and again one failed to explode. Four people were injured.

The following morning several aircraft unloaded a total of twenty-eight bombs;

A bomb which fell in Old Orchard Road on September 26, 1940, blew this crater in the road and fractured a water main but, fortunately, damage to homes was light.

two dropped eight HE between Cavendish Bridge and the station and The Avenue and two dropped sticks of ten each between Langney Road/Bourne Street and the area of Avondale Road/Nevill Road. At 4.35 that afternoon, a further eight bombs were dropped in the same general area — which soon earned the title 'Hell Fire Corner' — but the records have been lost. There were twenty-three injured.

In the early hours of Tuesday, September 24, three HE and two oil bombs were jettisoned on the town. Two HE were UXBs and one oil bomb failed to ignite. There were no casualties.

Two days later, on the afternoon of the 26th, seven HE and one oil bomb were dropped by two aircraft: four in the area of Cavendish Bridge/Station/St Leonard's Road and four in Old Orchard Road and Arlington Road. Two people were killed and two injured.

A salvo of four HE was dropped in the area about Cavendish Bridge and three HE and one oil bomb fell in the Cavendish Place/Tideswell Road/Bourne Street area. The bomb which demolished 69/71 Cavendish Place buried several people and rescue workers toiled unsparingly for thirty-six hours through daylight and darkness to reach the victims, knowing that only a short distance away a UXB lay in Mansfield's Garage. They had to tunnel and cut through obstructing concrete, hampered by water pouring from a burst main which required constant pumping to be kept in check.

During this rescue an emergency operation was performed under the debris to amputate the trapped legs of seventeen-year-old Peggy Harland and so release her. Throughout her ordeal, Peggy remained cheerful and constantly raised the morale of her rescuers, earning their undying respect for her outstanding courage. Regrettably, Peggy died in hospital on Monday the 30th. As a special tribute to her bravery, Peggy, a Girl Guide with the 1st Stone Cross Company, was posthumously awarded the Girl Guides' Gilt Cross for gallantry.

Others killed were Mr Stanley Giles, Mrs Olive Giles and Mrs Myrtle Wilkinson; fourteen people were injured.

The rescuers earned thirteen decorations or commendations. Chief Officer S.A. Phillips (Eastbourne Fire Brigade) was made an MBE; A.E. Blackmer, E.H. May and E.F. Stevens (Rescue Party) received the George Medal. Commendations went to: Dr J. Fenton (Medical Officer of Health); Dr R.M. Barron (First Aid Commandant); Dr L.A.H. Snowball (Surgeon); R.V. Harvey (Rescue); Sub-Officer S.N. Waymark (Fire Brigade); E.A. Homewood, (Fire Brigade); Constable R.J. Jeffrey; H.M. Barnes (Senior Air Raid Warden); A.J. Barkham (Warden).

During these few weeks air raid warnings rarely coincided with the actual raids and people began re-

The scene at the junction of Cavendish Place and Tideswell Road on September 28, 1940, when several people were trapped and an emergency amputation was performed beneath the debris to release Miss Peggy Harland. Sheer courage and devotion to duty became a by-word in this incident.

lying on their swiftly attuned hearing rather than any officially approved source. After the war some, who had not been in the town, doubted the ability of residents to distinguish friendly aero-engines from enemy ones but the fact remains that the faculty existed and saved many a life. Even so there was mounting pressure for warnings to be sounded locally on the advice of the Observer Corps. Alas, the Regional Controller, sitting thirty miles away, refused to hand over his responsibility and so attacks went unheralded — or the sirens would sound the alarm just as the enemy departed or even half-an-hour later.

The local Press, led by Tom Palmer, editor of the Eastbourne Gazette and Herald, fought a long-drawn-out campaign for a locally managed system and they were joined in this by the Mayor, Councillor (later Alderman) Rush and the Town Clerk, Mr Busby, but for a long time to come their combined efforts were strenuously resisted and Eastbournians continued to rely on their ears.

Bombed out of their Willoughby Crescent home, Jack and Gabi Hutchinson exemplify the indomitable spirit of the town as they salvage their belongings on a handcart.

The scene, looking west along Tideswell Road near the Cavendish Place junction, on September 28, 1940, when a number of people were trapped beneath the debris and rescue work continued for over forty-eight hours in extreme difficulties and with an unexploded bomb only a few yards away. This rescue resulted in more awards for gallantry than any other in Eastbourne during the war.

Bombs fall all autumn

WITHOUT ANY SEMBLANCE of anti-aircraft defences for the town and with the RAF unable to respond to the average lone attacker striking swiftly at the coast, it seemed that the German pilots could take their time and bomb almost at will. Indeed, on a number of occasions when the sky was clear, Dorniers could be seen on horizontal bombing runs with their flaps and undercarriages down. This apparent freedom of action, slow approach and the generally haphazard nature of the bombing combined to convince many residents that the town was being used as a practical training ground for the Luftwaffe's less experienced pilots and bomb-aimers. Right or wrong in this supposition, the impression has remained strong.

On Wednesday, October 2, 1940, at 6.45 in the morning, one of the regular Dornier loads of three large HE and one oil bomb fell in Upperton Gardens and Upperton Road, injuring twelve people. At 4.58pm the same day, another Do17 dropped the alternative load of a stick of smaller bombs in the South Street, Carlisle Road, Grassington Road, Silverdale Road and Blackwater Road area. Two people were killed and two injured. A further raid at 8.10pm near St Anthony's Avenue did no damage.

Two high explosive and one oil bombs were recorded when a Dornier Do17 struck at Northbourne Road at 10.30am on October 6. The inevitable third HE was never found. One person was injured in this attack. On the following day, a four-bomb load was dropped on the Enys Road, Bedford Grove, Carew Road area, injuring five people and causing superficial damage to the main entrance of the Princess Alice Memorial Hospital.

Bombers attacked three times on Tuesday, October 8. At 4.15pm one HE struck Lismore Road, two oil bombs caused fires in Terminus

Road property and a UXB fell in the rear garden of a small house in North Street. The latter was later dug out by a bomb disposal squad, every phase of the task being photographed by Wilf Bignell of the Eastbourne Gazette and Herald — regrettably, these pictures now appear to be lost. At 5.08pm another Dornier dropped two HE and two oil bombs between Hartington Place and Cavendish Place; then, at 6.45pm, eight HE were dropped between Cavendish Bridge and the Station. One of these penetrated the bridge carriageway and exploded in the space below, doing comparatively little damage. In all, one person died and three were injured during the day.

Two days later, at 3.30 on Thursday, October 10, a high-flying Dornier dropped four HE in a widely-spaced stick across Hampden Park. Bombs landed in playing fields, Park Avenue, Kings Drive and one demolished the church of St Mary-in-the-Park, Decoy Drive, leaving only the end wall with bell housing standing. Fortunately, only one person was injured.

The picture changed somewhat on the following day, Friday, when, at noon, two high-flying aircraft dropped a reported nine bombs over a wide area. One stick fell between Firle Road and the Saffrons Cricket Ground and the other was scattered across the levels between Lottbridge Drove and Rodmill. This second stick reputedly contained five bombs but it is likely that an old crater was mistakenly counted with the rest.

One bomb in the first stick stick fell on 94, 96 and 98 Sydney Road trapping a number of furniture removal men who were rescued by Mr John Hollands, who was injured, and Mr John Appleby. Mr Hollands was awarded an MBE and Mr Appleby was commended. Casualties for the day were

Bobbys (now Debenhams) sustained a near miss at its Lismore Road frontage on October 8, 1940.

Damage to the rear of a pair of semi-detached houses in Northbourne Road when a bomb fell in the gardens on October 6, 1940.

three dead and five injured.

After far less significant raids on October 13, 14, 17 and 19, unidentified aircraft attacked on the 22nd and, as the regional all-clear was sounding, reportedly dropped eleven large HE bombs, four of which fell on Langney Road and Bourne Street, doing considerable damage. A gas main was fractured in Langney Road and the gas ignited. Mr Francis Bates, Mr Hans Jensen and Mr John Bontoft were killed in this raid and fifteen injured. Three days later, on the 25th, a formation of enemy aircraft was attacked at a great height over the town by RAF fighters. As bombs fell in a line from The Goffs to Ringwood Road, the all-clear was sounded on the orders of the Regional Controller. One bomb in The Goffs practically demolished three houses and Inspector E. (Teddy) Winn, RSPCA, crawled through the wreckage to rescue a trapped dog. Afterwards he went to the hospital to report its safety to its mistress, injured in the raid. In all, six people were injured in this attack.

At 8.50pm on October 26, a Dornier Do17 struck the roof of a train standing at the station with an oil bomb which failed to ignite; a 250kg UXB lodged under the same train and was later defused. Two more UXBs fell in Kilburn Terrace (near the present multi-storey car park entrance). Only one of the latter was reported and the other only came to light during the afternoon when it exploded, killing Police Sergeant Dennis Owens and Sergeant Hoare of the bomb disposal squad. During subsequent efforts to rescue the two men, the reported bomb was found defused — it was the unknown bomb that had done the damage. In all, four people died that day.

There followed six attacks of little consequence on October 29, November 5, 6, 7 and 8 and in the early hours of Sunday, November 10. However, later that morning, at 10.10am, several bombers dropped at least twenty-eight bombs. Five fell in the sea, four on marshland behind Astaire Avenue and a reported nineteen made a long line from near the Albion Hotel and directly on the Lion Inn, to Dennis Road (now Dursley Road). Two sticks of ten made up this number (another bomb fell in the sea) and they overlapped somewhere near Langney Road. This was an attack made in good weather and the

A 250kg bomb took the front out of the Berkeley Club in Trinity Place on October 8, 1940 — a day when the town was raided three times in one afternoon.

RSPCA Inspector Teddy Winn rescues a pet dog from the rubble of its home. Whenever animals were in danger, Teddy Winn was quickly on the scene, frequently placing his own life on the line in his efforts to save the animals.

bombs which fell behind Astaire Avenue could be clearly seen as they flicked from the aircraft. Two people, one of whom was Mr Charles Rich, licensee of the Lion Inn, were killed and five were injured.

Two days later, a Dornier Do17, flying west to east at almost rooftop height, machine-gunned the streets and made out to sea — rumour had it that the aircraft later crashed in the Channel. Early on the evening of the same day (November 12, 1940) an enemy aircraft dropped at least twelve bombs through the Old Town council estate from near Ratton to Victoria Gardens. Not one bomb exploded. Most fell in gardens but one passed right through 16 Central Avenue from top to bottom, burying itself in the scullery floor. Four hundred people were evacuated from their homes until the bombs were declared safe.

Again rumour provided what of-ficialdom could not — it was said the the bombs had been made in Czechoslovakia and had been deliberately sabotaged! Alas, it is more likely that the bomb-aimer omitted to 'arm' the bombs before releasing them.

Seven more bombs are recorded as having fallen between Willingdon Road (where houses were damaged) and Kings Drive on November 15. Only a few people were hurt since, fortunately, much of the area, other than Willingdon Road and Kings Drive, was uninhabited in those days.

Friday, November 22, brought the last raid of consequence in 1940 when an aircraft (probably a Dornier Do17 or Do217) emerged from low cloud and dropped a long stick of bombs from the railway station to the beach near the Central Bandstand. This raid was generally known as 'The Pub Crawl' because

All that remained of St Mary's Church, Hampden Park, after a direct hit by a 250kg bomb on October 10, 1940. Tattered remains of prayer books and hymnals were found as far away as The Hydneye, east of the railway lines.

Above: Dennis (now Dursley) Road, at its junction with Winter (now Winchcombe) Road, sustained severe damage during a raid on September 23, 1940. *Right:* Mr Charles Rich, licensee, was killed and his wife was injured when a large bomb destroyed the Lion Inn on Sunday morning, November 10, 1940. *Below:* The result of a bomb on 4 and 6 The Goffs, on October 25, 1940.

Above: Damage to Cornfield Road shops inflicted in 'The Pub Crawl' raid on November 22, 1940. The premises on the right are now occupied by Stacey Marks, art dealers. *Left:* Langney Road on October 22, 1940, when an unusual number of bombs were dropped. *Below:* A bomb fell on platform 1 and the track at Eastbourne station, November 22, 1940, just as sirens sounded the 'all clear'.

Rescue squads and firemen from the adjacent auxiliary fire station labour on the debris of houses in Churchdale Road, destroyed on March 28, 1941.

the first obvious damage was to the Gildredge Hotel, while a damaged bomb ended up literally stuck through a panel of the door of the saloon bar of the Cavendish Hotel where it failed to explode. Mrs M.A. Graham was killed and ten people were injured.

Apart from a few inconsequential raids before Christmas, the town was left licking its wounds until March 12, 1941, when four bombs fell in the Northbourne Road/Churchdale Road area and two more were recorded at Halton Road and near the Angles Hotel.

Sweeping across the town at 500ft, on March 28 at 9.39am, a single Dornier Do17 dropped four HE bombs in the Archery area from Churchdale Road to Southbourne Road near its junction with Seaside. The first three hit houses in Churchdale Road, gardens behind them and houses in Willoughby Crescent. A deep indentation was found in Churchdale Road carriageway where a bomb had bounced and this explains the wide space between the first three and the last when they exploded. Later, bouncing bombs from low-flying aircraft became far less of a phenomenon, the short delay fuses enabling the aircraft to get clear before the explosions. Mrs A. Guy, Mrs A.M. Cooper and Brian Fly,

aged six, were killed and twenty-five people were injured.

Four HE bombs were dropped on the Crumbles between Princes Park and Langney Point on the evening of April 3, causing no damage. On the 9th, a single bomb was jettisoned on a military minefield on the Crumbles and later that day a single

The end of 'The Pub Crawl' raid — November 22, 1940 — an unexploded bomb in the door of the Cavendish Hotel.

Three large bombs cut a swathe through houses in Churchdale Road and Willoughby Crescent on March 28, 1941. A fourth bomb dropped by the Dornier Do17 bounced to within 100 yards of St Andrew's (Norway) Church before exploding.

raider dropped four HE bombs between Clifton Nurseries, Kings Drive and Little Ratton, doing minor damage and causing two slight casualties. An early morning attack took place on April 11, when a low-flying Dornier dropped four HE bombs in the Gildredge Park/Vicarage Drive area, causing only slight damage.

In the early hours of May 9, four HE bombs were dropped close to the locomotive sheds north of Whitley Road bridge; one failed to explode and rail services were delayed for twelve hours. Before re-starting services, Southern Railway shunted a line of trucks between the UXB and the main line. There was damage to locomotive sheds, sidings and the main line, also to electricity and telephone services.

Two more minor sorties were made during the early hours of May 11 but a third at 5.19am saw a Heinkel He111 drop eight HE bombs along Kings Drive, fortunately causing no casualties.

On Saturday, May 24, 1941, at 6.30pm, a Dornier swept low across the Archery area from north-west to south-east, dropping four HE bombs on Churchdale Road, Channel View Road and on the beach near Princes Park. Again an indentation in the carriageway beside the Archery Tavern indicated a bouncing bomb, the ten-second delay presumably carrying the bomb to Channel View Road before exploding. Fifteen people were injured in this attack.

The end of the first stage of Eastbourne's ordeal came when, on June 7, 1941, at 3.30am, a single raider came over the town with its engines throttled back and dropped four HE bombs before revving-up and climbing away. The bombs fell in a tight salvo in The Avenue and St Leonard's Road. Twelve people were injured.

No-one realised it at the time, and certainly no one expected it, but there ensued almost eleven months of comparative peace in the town, during which no air raids were recorded. Indeed, so quiet did Eastbourne become that a large number of people who had evacuated in September 1940 deemed it safe to return to their homes to tell of their hardships in their retreats...

The scene in Terminus Road looking towards the station on November 22, 1940. The shops on the right, now numbers 41/43, took a direct hit; centre is a large crater in front of what is now C&H Fabrics and in the background is the Gildredge Hotel which also took a direct hit.

As the bombs fell

This couple had only just taken their wedding vows at All Saints Church on August 15, 1940, when the sirens sounded. The vicar led the wedding party into the crypt for safety and the register was signed underground. The all-clear did not sound until 6pm when the couple emerged to go straight to their belated reception.

A Head Warden labours beneath the debris of a demolished house in Willoughby Crescent.

The fighter bombers

IT WAS FIVE minutes to two on the afternoon of Monday, May 4, 1942, when suddenly nine Messerschmitt Me109 fighters, each carrying a 250kg bomb and firing its cannon and machine-guns, swept low over the sea below the radar and raced across the town from the Holywell area, dropping their bombs in one of the most scattered attacks to date. The temporary lull was broken with a vengeance.

St John's Church, Meads, was hit and gutted by fire. Other bombs struck houses in Willingdon Road; the railway station; Commercial Road; the railway near Cavendish Bridge; the coal wharf (now Sandell Perkins yard) behind Winter Road (now Winchcombe Road); the east wing of the Cavendish Hotel; the locomotive sheds; the main gas holder at the gasworks at the far end of Gas Works Road (now Finmere Road). Mrs Henrietta Wise, Mrs Winifred Matthews, Mrs Mary Richardson, Mr Claude Benjamin and one other were killed and thirty-six people were injured.

A small fishing boat manned by Alec Huggett and Micky Andrews of Eastbourne was shot-up by the retreating fighters' cannon and machine-gun fire and both men were seriously injured. Local anger knew no bounds when, at 9.15 that same evening, William Joyce (the infamous 'Lord Haw-Haw') announced in his 'news in English' from Hamburg and Bremen, that German fighters had attacked an 'armed trawler' off Eastbourne.

A powerful new feature of this raid — apart from the fire-power of the fighters being turned against ordinary people — was that almost every bomb did serious damage. In general, the fighter pilots with their medium-capacity bombs looked to have a better aim than their comrades in the standard medium bombers.

On May 7, four more Messerschmitt Me109s attacked at 3.11pm,

An example of the damage cause by blast: shattered windows and boarded-up shopfronts in Grove Road.

dropping their 250kg bombs on Victoria Place (now re-named and re-numbered in an also re-numbered Terminus Road); the railway goods yard; the coal wharf behind Winter Road (Winchcombe Road); and the sea wall opposite Bolsover Road. Cannon and machine-guns were again used and Mr J. Payne was

The east wing of the Cavendish Hotel was shattered by a 250kg bomb from a Me109 fighter-bomber on May 4, 1942.

killed and thirty-one people were injured. Roy Hudson, photographer, whose premises in Victoria Place were demolished, lost many negatives and prints of previous raid damage. This site is being rebuilt at last, probably the last bombed site to be tidied up.

Just as this new type of assault was getting into its stride, the long-awaited local warning system was brought into operation — a victory over bureaucracy — and the 'cuckoo' could at last announce the imminent arrival of the enemy without reference to regional control.

Oddly enough, it was the conventional bombers which returned on August 11, 1942, at 11pm, to make one of the few deliberate night attacks on the town. The number of aircraft involved is uncertain but, as the largest number of HE bombs recorded is forty-seven and they were all large, it is probable that if Dorniers were again used there could have been up to a dozen.

The Upperton area bore the brunt; St Anne's Church was set ablaze and gutted before morning. The Grassington Road and College Road area was also heavily hit as was Grove Road and the railway station. Five unexploded bombs were recorded in the Upperton area. Additionally, there were reports of bombs in Arundel Road, Ashford

The devastated east wing of the Cavendish Hotel, struck by a bomb on May 4, 1942. RAF personnel were stationed there at the time.

Road, Gaudick Road, Compton Place, Compton Place Road and on the Royal Eastbourne Golf Course. Mapped bomb strikes tend to bear out all the reports.

Some 2,000 2kg thermite incendiary bombs were dropped, many of them fitted with burster charges timed to explode after the main filling had ignited, scattering blazing fragments to spread the fire and to keep away firefighters. However, those bombs which were not already out of hand were soon dealt with by adaptable people, including Canadian soldiers, who tossed sandbags on them to damp down the explosive effect and contain the fire.

Civilian casualties included Mrs Mary Taylor, Mrs W.E. Walker and Miss S. Boucher, who were killed, as were eight Canadian RAMC men. The

St John's Church, Meads, fell victim to the first fighter-bomber raid — May 4, 1942. It was shattered and set ablaze so that all that remained was the shell and charred timber.

The neighbouring railway sidings and station resulted in many bombs falling on commercial premises behind St Leonard's Road and Commercial Road. This one fell on wine merchants Fremlins on May 4, 1942.

The vital air raid warnings now included the local 'cuckoo' alarm.

injured numbered nine, including three Canadians.

One enemy aircraft was seen ablaze as it crossed the east end of the town on its way home.

In the front garden of a house in Upper Avenue, a tree took a direct hit on the top of its trunk from a 250kg bomb and was hacked down to a tall stump with a splintered top. This tree still survives and, in summer leaf, shows no sign of having suffered in any way; only in winter can any indication be seen as to which tree it is.

A number of questions arose over this particular raid: the sheer weight of the attack; its principal target area; the use of flares to ensure it got home in the right location; and the date. It came just prior to the ill-fated Dieppe raid about which so much controversy has raged over a suggested intelligence leak. Canadian troops had long been billeted in the town and it was Canadian 2nd Infantry Division troops who were to compose the main body of the attacking force at Dieppe. This was not only the most severe night raid on the

A 250kg bomb did this damage to Victoria Place (now the seaward end of Terminus Road) on May 7, 1942. The site was the last in the town to be fully redeveloped.

The gutted remains of St Anne's Church, Upperton Gardens, destroyed by incendiary bombs on the night of August 11, 1942, after surviving several near misses earlier in the war.

During the night raid on August 11, 1942, a bomb exploded in the front garden of 13 St Anne's Road, felling trees and causing blast damage.

The scene after two bombs fell on Pevensey on August 14, 1942.

One of four Focke-Wulfe FW190s caused this scene of destruction at Pevensey Bay on August 13, 1942, after its bomb struck the newsagents' roof and bounced into the garage at the rear. Two of the planes went on to Eastbourne where a gasholder was badly damaged.

town but there was a deliberate intention to saturate a particular area.

Two days later, early on Thursday, August 13, 1942, four Focke-Wulfe FW190 fighter-bombers crossed the coast near Cooden and turned westward. Two dropped their 500kg bombs at Pevensey Bay then turned for home while the remaining pair came on to Eastbourne, raking the town with cannon fire and dropping one bomb near a gasholder, holing it and igniting the gas. The second bomb fell in Roseveare Road. Two people were injured.

Almost a fortnight later, at 8.53 on the morning of Wednesday, August 26, two Focke-Wulfe FW190s came in over the coast. One dropped its 500kg bomb on Marlow Avenue, destroying several houses, and the other's bomb fell on the Eastbourne Corporation Electricity Generating Station (now the site of the amenity dump and destructor works off St Philip's Avenue and Churchdale Road). Mr Frank Moore, a Corporation employee, was killed outright and Mrs Lucy Dann and Mrs Ruth Chatfield of Marlow Avenue died in hospital. Seven people were injured.

Enys Road houses shattered by bombs on the night of August 11, 1942, when the Upperton area suffered the worst night attack of the war.

An auxiliary ambulance waits while rescuers labour to release trapped people in the rubble of the Alexandra Arms, Seaside, after a single Dornier dropped four bombs in a tight salvo on October 26, 1942.

Two Focke-Wulfe FW190 fighter-bombers attacked Marlow Avenue — pictured here — and the electricity generating station in Churchdale Road on August 26, 1942. One of the attackers was shot down into a ditch beside the original Lottbridge Drove.

A casualty detector unit was used for the first time after four bombs hit Marks and Spencer and other buildings in Terminus Road on December 18, 1942. Here rescuers follow 'silent routine' as microphones are used to listen for the sound of survivors.

One of the fighters crashed into a ditch at the side of the old Lottbridge Drove (west of the axis of the modern road). It was shot down by a Canadian Bren-gunner who fired a long burst at the attackers as they swept across his front from left to right; it was later observed that there was a bullet hole in the cockpit canopy of the wrecked aircraft.

After a three-week respite, two Focke-Wulfe FW190s came in very low on Wednesday, September 16, at 11.52am, and made for the station. Only one carried a 500kg bomb which it dropped on No 1 platform. The bomb then ricocheted into 'the passenger dock' where it exploded. The two aircraft then fired on Whitley Road, Annington Road, Beach Road and Seaford Road on their way out. Six people were killed, nine seriously injured and twenty-seven slightly hurt.

There followed another long break — more than a month — until, at 1pm on Monday, October 26, a Dornier Do217 crossed the town from west to east at 500ft with its guns going and dropped four 250kg bombs, one on Willoughby Crescent and three in Seaside's 'Norway' area, between Southbourne Road and Lottbridge Drove. The Alexandra Arms was destroyed and a bus severely damaged.

In Willoughby Crescent, Mr and Mrs William Ripley, their son David (14) and Mrs Ethel Boniface, were killed. In their home in Seaside, Mrs Beatrice Sherwood and her children, Joan (10) and Keith (5), died. Mr Samuel Marley, a bus driver, was also killed. Fatally injured were: Mr Mortimer Boniface, Mr Charles Burgess, Douglas Gower (13), Mr Grayson Baker, Mrs F.M. Grant, Mrs Rose Gearing and Louise Burtenshaw (15). In all, fifteen died and twenty-two were injured.

Several people were buried in the ruins of the Alexandra Arms and a lorry was set on fire and burnt-out. Many houses suffered severe damage and the church of St Andrew (Norway) suffered badly from blast.

Such a heavy casualty list resulting from one aircraft carrying

Rescue workers take a breather during work on the shattered remains of Marks and Spencer after a tight salvo caused heavy casualties and damage on December 18, 1942.

only four bombs was shattering enough and must have made many returned evacuees wish they had stayed away but, almost two months later, this grim total was exceeded...

Even with the exigencies of war, rationing and desperate shortages of the good things of life, Christmas held a certain amount of its old magic and the struggle to provide seasonal fare and gifts was still a feature of the pre-Christmas season. The streets and shops were busy with Christmas shoppers when, at noon on Friday, December 18, 1942, a Dornier Do217 flew low amid cloud and rain and dropped a salvo of four 500kg HE bombs near the town centre. The bombs fell in such close company that there were even claims that they had been chained together to gain the added effect of a compound explosion — but that must be regarded as pure speculation and the likelihood is that the salvo had no height in which to deploy farther.

One bomb was a direct hit on 45 and 47 Terminus Road (now 139 and 141 since re-numbering); one bomb made a direct hit on 49 Terminus Road (now part of 133/137); and two bombs fell directly on Marks and Spencer, 51 and 53 Terminus Road (now 133/137). Neighbouring shops were also devastated and, listing the shops on their original numbering and names, they were: 41, Terminus Road Post Office (often erroneously referred to as 'Langney Road Post Office' — Langney Road begins at the lane beside the Job-Centre); 43, John Duke, tailor and outfitter; 45, Eastbourne Artisans' and Labourers' Improved Dwellings Co; 47, Dr Scholl's Foot Comfort Service plus two dentists' surgeries; 49, General Accident Fire and Life Assurance; 51 and 53, Marks and Spencer Ltd.

Many people were buried beneath a mountain of debris and there was great difficulty in extricating them — so much so that specialist assistance was called in under the ARP mutual aid scheme and a casualty detector unit was used

Rescuers turn their heads skywards as they hear aircraft engines while they struggle to free people buried under the rubble of Marks and Spencer.

Just part of the havoc created by four bombs on Marks and Spencer and neighbouring premises in Terminus Road while people were doing their Christmas shopping on December 18, 1942. Relays of rescuers worked non-stop for 24 hours to release those trapped and recover the bodies of others. Eighteen people died and thirty-seven were injured.

for the first time in Eastbourne. The local rescue people performed magnificently, assisted by reinforcements from Bexhill and Hastings (two parties); Kent Mobile Reserve (two parties); Tunbridge Wells, Hove, Lewes and Hailsham.

Additionally, maximum assistance was forthcoming from Canadian 1st Infantry Division (its 2nd Infantry Brigade was stationed locally at the time); 2nd Light Anti-Aircraft Regiment RCA; 2nd Field Regiment RCA; Princess Patricia's Canadian Light Infantry; 569 Army Troops, RE; 185 Pioneer Group, RE; also ET School, RAF, and 21st (Eastbourne) Battalion, Sussex Home Guard.

The rescue work continued tenaciously for forty-eight hours under conditions so difficult as to result in a further nine casualties from falling debris.

Those killed were: Mr Theobald Vinsen (dentist), Mr J.P. Smith, Mrs Eva Nicholls, Michael Nicholls (nine months), Mrs Daisy Gurr, Miss Jessie Cockburn, Mrs Edith Anker, Mrs Emily Randall, Miss Kate Willson, Mrs Emily Packham, Jean Turner (11), Mrs Marjorie Bowen, Mrs Florrie Selway, Mrs

Ethel Hart, Miss Anna Bonner, Mrs Edith Scott, Mrs Beatrice Chambers and Mrs Eliza White.

In all, eighteen people died and thirty-seven were injured.

It fell to the fighter-bombers to complete the year's work for the Luftwaffe when, on Tuesday, December 29, at 2.56pm, two Focke-Wulfe FW190s swept across the town from the west and, with guns blazing, dropped two 500kg bombs. One first struck the ground in the allotments off Longland Road, bounced over Longland and Dillingburgh Roads, passed through 67 Victoria Drive and exploded in number 62 across the street. The total distance from first strike to explosion is estimated in excess of 200 yards — the bouncing bomb phenomenon was not new, of course, but this example is one of the more notable. The second bomb landed in gardens at the rear of the 'Court House', Moat Croft Road.

Mrs Charlotte Dry was killed and Mrs Harriett Marchant died in hospital. Thirty-six people were injured.

1942 was at an end but the New Year was to bring little, if any, weakening of the enemy attacks.

Teams of rescue workers in the remains of a house in Victoria Drive — bombed on December 29, 1942.

The biter bit

Above: This Messerschmitt Me109, crash-landed near Beachy Head on May 23, 1942.
Left: Photographer Harry Deal pictured by Wilf Bignell with the remains of the twin-engined Messerschmitt Me110 fighter which fell into the grounds of Aldro School after being shot down on August 16, 1940, over Meads. The pilot's body fell onto the roof of nearby Hill Brow School while the gunner parachuted into the sea and drowned.

A ditch beside Lottbridge Drove (the original drove road) makes the last resting place for a Focke-Wulfe FW190 fighter-bomber shot down by a Canadian Bren-gunner on August 26, 1942. Unfortunately, it had already dropped its 500kg bomb and caused casualties and damage.

A Messerschmitt Me109 fighter downed in a cornfield at Berwick during the Battle of Britain (August 12, 1940). The pilot's boots were taken away to hamper any escape bid. Note the red devil painted on the nose of the light blue plane.

Above: Two soldiers stand guard over another Me109 which made a belly landing near Eastbourne on September 30, 1940. This plane survived the war and was flown in North America before being returned to this country in 1966 for restoration. *Left:* The Messerschmitt's tailplane showing the pilot's five 'kills' dated May 13 (two), 18 and 24 and June 14, 1940. *Below:* A Messerschmitt Me110 which crash-landed at Hooe on August 15, 1940, is guarded by troops pending removal by RAF personnel.

A young couple find the bath and gas water heater the only notable remaining features — yet they remain cheerful.

The crew of a 40mm Bofors anti-aircraft gun drill on the flat roof of the Pier Pavilion (now the Blue Room).

Barclays Bank, Terminus Road — together with John Pring's furnishers — was destroyed by a 500kg bomb on March 7, 1943.

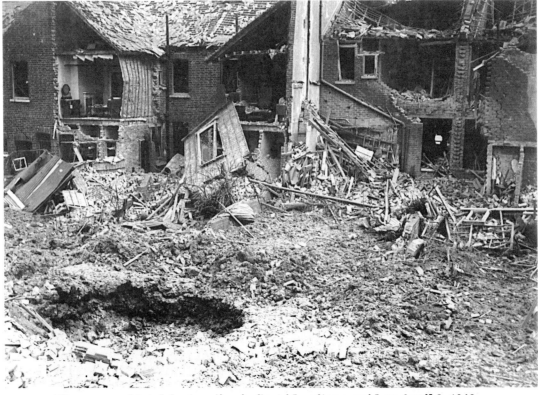

The scene of total destruction in Seaside after a raid on April 3, 1943.

It's back to square one

IT WAS BACK to 'square one' on Friday, January 15, 1943 when, at two in the afternoon — and without any prior warning from the sirens — four Focke-Wulfe FW190s again crossed the town from the west, firing cannon and dropping one 500kg bomb each. One bomb struck 33 and 35 Green Street; one hit 3/4 Wilmington Terrace; one landed in a passageway between the Imperial Hotel, Devonshire Place, and Hartington Place; and the fourth fell in a cleared area of Cross Street and Duke Street (just off Bourne Street and Langney Road — behind the Rose and Crown public house — and partly included in a school playground). Earlier in the bombing campaign, that area had become known as 'Hell Fire Corner' because so many sticks and salvos of bombs fell there or crossed the district and this last bomb completed the destruction so effectively executed by the others.

The reason there was no local (cuckoo) warning sounded for this raid was that the sirens had been knocked out by a storm.

The most serious damage was done at Wilmington Terrace where it took twenty-four hours to extricate people trapped beneath the debris, but the effort was rendered futile when it was found that they were all dead.

One man was struck by a machine-gun bullet while in the street and he died in hospital.

The total toll of dead in this raid was: Mr F. Gosden, Mrs Frances Crowhurst, Miss Louisa Crowhurst, Mr A.J. Kelly, Mr Joseph Rayner, Mrs Daisy Rayner, Lily Jackson, Mr J. Steed, Mrs Matilda Hughes and Mrs Lily Arnold. Thirty-eight people were injured.

A machine-gun and cannon attack was made on the town on Saturday, January 23 when four Focke-Wulfe FW190s dropped their bombs in the Eastern, Central and Western Avenues area of Polegate, demol-

Duke Street and Cross Street were part of the area backing Bourne Street and Langney Road and, as such, suffered more than their fair share of the bombing so that they formed part of a single, broad devastated area known as 'Hell Fire Corner'. To add insult to injury, on January 15, 1943, a fighter-bomber dropped a 500kg bomb in the area and finished off the task of demolition.

The fearful destruction caused by a 500kg bomb which fell on 33 and 35 Green Street, Old Town, on January 15, 1943.

ishing several bungalows and causing fatal casualties. The planes then ran for home, raking Old Town, Eastbourne, with cannon and machine-gun fire on their way. No casualties occurred in the town but the enemy did not get away scot-free — a Bofors gun crew at Cow Gap claimed one enemy aircraft shot down in the sea and later wreckage and the body of a German airman were washed up to confirm their claim.

On Sunday, February 7, 1943, at 2.47pm, four more Focke-Wulfe FW190s each dropped a 500kg bomb as they swept across the town. One HE scored a direct hit on the Central Fire Station, Grove Road (now part of the Grove Road wing of the Borough Treasurer's Department); one struck 126/130 Terminus Road (now 62, 64 and 66 since re-numbering); one landed in Lushington Road and one in Hardwick Road.

The bombing of the Central Fire Station was a serious blow in itself for it was the headquarters of the local fire brigade — though there were, of course, many minor temporary fire stations dotted about the town and the service as a whole was not severely damaged.

The Lushington Road bomb passed through houses on one side of the street and burst on the other side, badly damaging three houses and partly damaging many others.

In all, nine members of the general public, six National Fire Service personnel (the local brigade and auxiliary fire service had been incorporated in one national force) and four soldiers were killed. Civilians: NFS — Section Leader J.W. Bailey, Leading Fireman Frederick Mewett, Firewoman Pearl Chitty, Firemen John Hunter, Frederick Duke and Walter Goacher; public — Miss Emily Pringle, Miss Florence Norman, Mrs Ruth Cree, Miss Emily Taylerson, Miss Ellen Tydeman and Miss Evelyn Wilson. Some seventy-two people, civilian

A council workman has handed the Town Clerk, Mr Francis H. Busby (right), a photograph of a smiling Winston Churchill, found undamaged in the wreckage of a house in Lushington Road after a raid in 1943.

The rear of Eastbourne Central Fire Station, headquarters of the local brigade, suffered much blast damage before a 500kg bomb scored a direct hit on February 7, 1943. Five firemen and a firewoman were killed.

Russell and Bromley and Brufords, jewellers, of Terminus Road were destroyed by a 500kg bomb dropped by a Focke-Wulfe FW190 fighter-bomber during a raid on February 7, 1943.

Firemen search through the wreckage after the raid in which four FW190s, flying out of the sun at low altitude, bombed and machine-gunned the town on February 7, 1943, killing nineteen people and injuring seventy-two.

and armed forces personnel, were injured.

Again East Sussex and Kent sent rescue crews to assist and a casualty detector unit attended.

Uncharacteristically, two Dornier Do217s machine-gunned Meads, Old Town and Hampden Park on February 9 at 8.13am before proceeding inland but there were no casualties and only superficial damage to property.

March 7, 1943, and another punishing raid by fifteen assorted Messerschmitt Me109s and Focke-Wulfe FW190s which came in low across the sea at 12.52pm and climbed sharply to cross Beachy Head. Two FWs bombed early, one near the radar station and one in a ploughed field. All the aircraft then dived across the town where the remaining bomb carriers dropped their loads — the Me109s carried one 250kg bomb each and the FW190s each carried one 500kg bomb. One of the latter bombs broke up when it struck the chimney stack of 3 and 4 Harts Cottages, Meads, and also damaged numbers 2 and 5. A 250kg bomb bounced from the Longland Road area into Ocklynge Cemetery where it killed two people.

Other bombs destroyed 2, 4 and 6 New Upperton Road; Barclays Bank, Terminus Road (opposite Cornfield Road); 33, 35 and 37 Cornfield Road; a warehouse in Junction Road; 43, 45 and 47 Jevington Gardens; Mostyn Hotel, Grand Parade; 22, 24, 26 and 28 Meads Street; two 250kg bombs fell in gardens at 3 Staveley Road and 44 St John's Road.

Later, the Air Ministry claimed that two of the attackers had been shot down.

Those who died were: Mr William Payton, Mrs E. Payton, Miss Annie Hollebon, Miss Alice Hollebon, Mr Albert Newman, Mr Donald Mackay, Mrs Ellen Smith, Miss Violet Hipwell, Miss Henrietta Hollebon, Mr Cecil Blake, Mr Cornelius de la Roche, Miss M. Perry,

A 250kg bomb dropped by a Messerschmitt Me109 fighter-bomber destroyed 2, 4 and 6 New Upperton Road near its junction with Upperton Road on March 7, 1943.

Barclays Bank and Prings, furnishers, took the full force of a 500kg bomb dropped in Terminus Road by a Focke-Wulfe fighter-bomber on March 7, 1943.

The damage in Cornfield Road after a punishing raid by fifteen assorted
Messerschmitt and Focke-Wulfe fighter-bombers on March 7, 1943.

Meads Street suffered severe damage when houses were demolished in the March 7
raid.

Miss Auguston Currie and Mr David Gillies. Over fifty people were injured.

The records of a raid by fighter-bombers at 11.46am on Saturday, April 3, 1943, show that on this day occurred the worst-ever casualty figures for a single raid on the town. They also declare that ten assorted Me109s and FW190s dropped twelve bombs between them. Until this occasion, each fighter aircraft had carried only one bomb — 250kg or 500kg — but, in order to arrive at twelve bombs from ten aircraft, it would require two FW190s to carry two 250kg bombs apiece, or there was the introduction of the FW190A5/U3 which could carry two 250kg and one 500kg bombs. Which of these options was actually used is still unknown.

The Park Gates Hotel, Compton Street; 2 and 4 Burlington Place; 6 and 8 Terminus Road (now 194 and 196 since re-numbering); 2, 4, 6 and 8 Ceylon Place; 105/113 Tideswell Road; 29/37 Longstone Road; 83 and 85 Avondale Road; gardens behind 278 and 280 Seaside, all were hit by 500kg bombs. A bomb reputed to be a 250kg destroyed eight houses in Beltring Road/Firle Road — extraordinary damage for one of the smaller bombs — and a bomb of unknown size passed through the Whitehall Hotel, Howard Square,

and burst in the sea.

A 250kg bomb demolished Sussex House, Harding Mews, Wish Cottage and mews; another demolished a surface air raid shelter in Spencer Road. The shelter was of the brick wall and concrete roof variety erected just before or in the early days of the war, intended purely as a blast shelter for people caught out of doors during a raid. The 250kg bomb made a direct hit and literally destroyed it as a building. Several people inside were killed. In Terminus Road, near the junction with Seaside, a 500kg bomb destroyed several shops opposite Dale and Kerley's department store (now A & N) which was itself extensively damaged.

The scene in Spencer Road alongside St Saviour's Church after a surface blast shelter was destroyed on April 3, 1943.

The Park Gates Hotel, Compton Street, suffered severe damage during the April 3, 1943 raid by ten fighter-bombers, one of which dropped this 500kg bomb, tearing the centre out of the building.

A rubble-strewn road is all that remains to show where a surface blast shelter in Spencer Road took a direct hit from a 250kg bomb on April 3, 1943, killing those sheltering inside.

When a 500kg bomb struck 6 and 8 Terminus Road (now 194/196) on April 3, 1943, it trapped a number of people in a cellar shelter, fractured a gas main in the street and did considerable damage to Dale & Kerley's store (now A & N) opposite. Here, firemen damp down the blazing gas main until the gas can be cut off.

Another view of the destruction in Terminus Road when ten fighter-bombers attacked on April 3, 1943, causing the worst-ever casualty figures for a single raid on Eastbourne.

Bomb damage in Havelock Road sustained during an attack on June 4, 1943.

A view of the rear of the Central Library and Technical Institute which, having survived numerous smaller bombs and near misses, finally succumbed to this 500kg bomb dropped on June 4, 1943.

From a basement shelter beneath one of the smashed shops, a number of people were rescued, some of them injured. One of the bombs struck the pavement in Upper Avenue and bounced 200 yards before exploding.

The dead included: Mr Ethelbert Keay, Mr W.J. Edmonds, Mr Arthur Pidcock, Mr Ernest Mason, Miss F.L. Prodger, Miss Mary Brook, Mrs Mary Crisp, Peter Horton (8), Anthony Ellett (5), Mr Joseph Hutchinson, Mrs Alice Dobell, Miss A.K. Oliver, Mrs Eleanor Cherryman, Mrs Grace Prior, Mrs Ethel Elson, Mr Christopher Bonfiglioli, Mrs Dorothy Bonfiglioli, Miss Rose Lawrence, Mrs Ellen Williams, Miss Doris Hardwick, Betty Walker, Mrs Sarah Tidey, Mrs Edith McKinley, Miss Amy Bagshawe, Mrs E.L. Wilkins, Mrs Fanny Wren, Mrs F.W. van Mulbrecht, Mr Jacobus van Mulbrecht, Mrs Kathleen Davies, Mrs L.G. Thorne, Mrs Annie Colvin and Mr George Sargent. Some ninety-nine people were injured.

It was claimed that two of the attacking planes were themselves hit.

The next fighter-bomber attack came on June 4, 1943, at 11.28 on a Friday morning. It was a raid made by a large number of aircraft, reputedly all Focke-Wulfe FW190s, though their actual numbers are unknown because the ARP records of this attack have been lost. Variously, the figures are put at sixteen or eighteen aircraft which dropped thirteen or fourteen bombs. In fact, fourteen bombs were dropped, probably all of 500kg calibre.

An accurate listing is: a direct hit on the Technical Institute/Central Library, Grove Road (since rebuilt as the Borough Treasurer's Department and Library); Mac-Fisheries, Grove Road, now a restaurant; a UXB passed through St Saviour's Vicarage and lodged in the church; garages near Woodgate Road and St Philip's Avenue junction; Bowood Avenue; middle of the even numbers in Havelock Road; HE beside the old 'Hospital Block' in the Ordnance Yard (the block, long

The wreckage of this car shows graphically the dangers of blast damage.

Firemen play hoses to damp down a blazing gas main in Terminus Road opposite Dale and Kerley's (now A & N) when a bomb destroyed shops and buried a number of people sheltering in a cellar. The tall building in the background was Beales' department store, now owned by the Co-Op.

73

The destruction wrought at the Central Library during a large raid by up to eighteen aircraft on June 4, 1943.

since disused as a hospital, was HQ of 'C' Company, 21st Sussex Home Guard); Winter Road (now Winchcombe Road); houses in Southbourne Road; St Anthony's Avenue houses; Hotel Metropole at junction of Marine and Royal parades (now rebuilt as Metropole Court, flats); near Fishermen's Club, Royal Parade; an anti-aircraft gun site at Paradise Drive; Commercial Road.

Those who died were: Mr A. Leitch, Mrs Cecily Ashdown, Mrs Emily Simmonds, Mrs Lily Hylands, Mrs Mary Walters, Mrs J.E. Harries, Mr George Dorman and Mr William Freeman. Thirty-three were injured.

Two days later, at 1.38 on the afternoon of June 6, 1943 — precisely one year before D-Day and the invasion of Normandy — fourteen Focke-Wulfe FW190s made the last severe attack of the war on Eastbourne. All the bombs were of 500kg and damage was consequently high.

Crossing the coast at a height of thirty feet in the vicinity of Princes Park, the aircraft dropped: one bomb on the Crumbles (near the present Leisure Pool complex); in Princes Park near Channel View Road; 35/45 Beach Road; open ground near the gasworks; one passed through 13 and 15 Waterworks Road and demolished a cottage in the Waterworks Company's yard; Caffyns Garage, junction of Seaside and Seaside Road (now site of roundabout); 103/111 Ashford Road; 25 and 27 The Avenue; 27 St Anne's Road; 28/30 Lushington Road; 10 College Road; Beachlawn, Selwyn Road; 1 Pashley Road; Hildegarde, Meads Road.

Those killed were: Mr William Cromwell, Mr H.L. Longworth, Mr Harry Pinnington, Mrs E. Pinnington, Miss Annie Child, Mr Benjamin Hillidge, Mrs E. Chapman and several military policemen.

On their way home, some of the attackers fired on the Royal Observer Corps post on Beachy Head, peppering the wooden hut there with more than a hundred rounds from cannon and machine-guns.

The worst of Eastbourne's ordeal was, at last, over, although no-one was to know until a long time later and, for many months, ears and eyes were half-cocked for the first indications of a resumption of raids by Dorniers or the fighter-bombers — but there was a very different hazard to come...

The Metropole and Balmoral Hotels took the full force of a 500kg bomb, one of fourteen dropped during a raid on the June 4, 1943.

The scene at the bottom of Grove Road on June 4, 1943 when a 500kg bomb demolished several shops between Terminus Road and Ivy Terrace. *Top:* Rescuers toil amid the debris while *centre* an auxiliary ambulance stands by near the forlorn remains of a corporation bus awaiting recovery.

Caffyns large garage premises at the junction of Seaside and Seaside Road (now a roundabout) were destroyed by a 500kg bomb on June 6, 1943 — one year before D-Day.

The final phase

FIVE MINOR ATTACKS took place between July 30, 1943 and the end of the year. In four cases the bombs fell at night and struck open ground, but on December 30 at 7.10pm, four bombs fell in the Langney area — one near the Priory; one behind the abattoir (now the junction of Faversham Road and Langney Rise); one near the piggeries behind Langney Cemetery and a UXB near Fort Cottages, Pevensey Bay Road.

1944 opened in similar vein, with two very minor night raids. However, at five minutes to one in the early morning of Tuesday, March 14, three fighter-bombers made an uncharacteristic night raid. They crossed the coast near Langney Point in moonlight and with engines throttled back. After dropping two bombs, they opened up and made for home, dropping the third bomb in the sea.

One bomb fell near 13 St Anne's Road, damaging property and setting military vehicles ablaze; the other fell on the railway station, damaging tracks 2 and 3 and station buildings. Only one person was slightly hurt. Again in the small hours, a bomber dropped two bombs which struck 13 West Gardens and open ground behind West Crescent on March 22.

The last conventional bombs to fall within the boundaries of the County Borough of Eastbourne were probably dumped by a night bomber heading for home at 3.35 in the morning of March 31, 1944. Fortunately one fell on the Crumbles near Pevensey Bay Road and another adjoining Willingdon Golf Course.

The Allied armies went back into northern France on D-Day, June 6, 1944, and light could at last be glimpsed at the end of a long, dark tunnel...

Six days later, however, the picture changed when, at 4am on June 13, clear visibility enabled observers on Beachy Head to see, thirty miles away, the glowing tail of the first V1 'Flying Bomb', which fell in open country, causing no damage. Later that day a confidential message was received at the observer post stating that: 'The enemy last night used P.A.C. (Pilotless Air Craft).' A few nights later there were a few more — a trickle which rapidly became a stream.

Before the war a midget racing car for use on speedway tracks was introduced into England from America. Its American nickname was 'Doodle-Bug' — and this name was duly handed on to the flying bombs because of the noise peculiar to the V1's simple ram-jet engine. The harsh roar of the V1s was sustained until they reached their target when it would stop; the bomb would then simply dive to the ground and explode with devastating effect. When anti-aircraft guns only dis-

An uncharacteristic night raid on March 14, 1944 caused further damage to the railway station.

abled the V1s, however, the effect was much the same.

Thereafter, for two-and-a-half months, hundreds of V1s roared over the town on one or another of their numerous set routes — so stolidly as to appear to be running on rails. Realising that disabling the V1s over the outskirts of London was virtually playing the enemy's game, the risk of denuding the capital's air defences was accepted and, over a period of two or three days, masses of anti-aircraft guns were moved to the South Coast where they were grouped close to the established routes of the V1s.

As the flying bombs were spotted out to sea, a signal rocket would be fired by lookouts to indicate which route they were following and the guns would begin firing, their noise akin to a full-scale First World War artillery barrage. Long lines of smoke blobs from exploding shells traced the course of the V1s until there would suddenly appear a massive dark grey cloud with a red centre and the ram-jet engine would come cartwheeling out of the smoke as the V1 exploded in the air. Unfortunately, the bursting shells also created a serious hazard when shell-splinters (mis-named 'shrapnel') fell like hot steel rain on the built-up areas. Thereafter, attempts were made to hit the V1s over the sea.

Fighter pilots returning from supporting troops in Normandy also took a hand, spectacularly shooting down quite a number of V1s, but the piece-de-resistance was really the tactics of fighter pilots who, out of ammunition, would fly alongside a

A fighter-bomber dropped the bomb that tore up tracks between platforms 2 and 3 on March 14, 1943 — one of many occasions when the railway station sustained damage.

Another view of the damage inflicted at Eastbourne's railway station after the raid on
March 14, 1943.

V1, gently tilting its wingtip with that of their own aircraft until the V1 faced back the way it had come, its giroscope then holding it firmly to its new course — a matter for grim satisfaction for those watching from below.

On June 18, at 8.25pm, a Doodle-Bug, damaged by anti-aircraft fire, fell in the triangle of Charleston Road, Milton Road and Mountney Road. There was considerable damage over a wide area but, fortunately, no-one was killed, although forty-one people were injured and seven of the worst damaged houses subsequently had to be demolished.

Another damaged V1 fell at the west entrance to Hampden Park at 8.10 on the morning of June 22, de-

A rare visit to the town by an American army officer. He turned up to view the damage caused by a V1 on June 18, 1944.

stroying the thatched tea chalet and damaging the Park Keeper's lodge. Three people were hurt. Next day a V1 struck the cliff slope at Beachy Head, close to the signal station, radar station and Observer Corps post. And on June 27, just after midnight, another flying bomb hit the cliff face near the lighthouse.

On July 4 a fighter pilot intercepted a flying bomb as it approached the coast near the east end of the town but, before opening fire, he waited for the bomb to be near open country. Over Astaire Avenue, he gave the V1 a short burst but, in the manner of its kind, it dived straight into the ground at the rear of the avenue. Six houses had later to be demolished and much damage was caused to others. That night another V1 crashed near Tutts Barn Lane, doing little damage.

Six houses were demolished at Brassey Avenue, Hampden Park, at 7.25pm on July 27 and thirty-four people were injured. On August 1, fighters brought down another on the Downs but, at 3.40pm, a V1 exploded in the air over Old Town, damaging property and injuring three people. Two days later anti-aircraft fire exploded another in the air over Meads; fortunately, only superficial damage was done.

The triangle formed by Charleston, Milton and Mountney Roads bore the brunt when a V1 flying bomb shot down on June 18, 1944, exploded.

Flying bomb blast

The damage caused by the V1 shot down on June 18, 1944 was considerable. Although it was not a direct hit, several houses in Charleston, Milton and Mountney Roads were virtually destroyed or had to be demolished for safety reasons.

A V1 Flying bomb shot down behind Astaire Avenue on July 4, 1944 caused tremendous blast damage to houses which subsequently had to be demolished.

On August 7 at 11.16pm a damaged and burning Doodle-Bug crossed the coast near Holywell and, despite the claim that its engine had stopped, it managed to descend slowly, eventually crashing in Baldwin Avenue, behind St Elisabeth's Church, demolishing some houses in Baldwin Avenue and damaging others over a wide area. Seven days later, as the British Army advanced behind the French coast, the last flying bomb to be destroyed immediately over the town exploded near Holywell.

The fact that so few V1s are recorded here should not be taken to indicate that only a few were despatched from France, destroyed by the guns sited around the town's perimeter, or by the RAF and, on occasion, the USAAF. Hundreds came in along the set courses; many were hit and exploded in the air or on the sea or land; others crashed in their hundreds farther north in Sussex and the number reaching the capital — large though it was — was very much less than it otherwise would have been. A glance at the map of flying bomb landfalls will suffice to show how the south-east absorbed much of the shock intended for London.

An unexploded fire bomb of the sort rained on Eastbourne.

The rocket motor of a V2 ballistic rocket. Supersonic, these missiles exploded ahead of the sound of their approach and no warning of them was possible.

Victory at last!

Above: Wrens and Artificers from HMS Marlborough (Eastbourne College) link arms outside the Town Hall as they celebrate the ending of the war in Europe: VE Day, May 9, 1945. *Left:* Soldiers, a girl and a sailor celebrate VE Day with a drink at a window of the Burlington Hotel bar (now Burlington Bertie's). *Below:* A huge assembly of townspeople gathered at the Bandstand to give thanks for the ending of the war with Japan — VJ Day, August 15, 1945.

Credit where credit's due

UNDOUBTEDLY THERE WERE innumerable Eastbourne people deserving of praise for courage and devotion to duty but, as mentioned at the outset, Councillor (later Alderman) Arthur Rush and the Town Clerk, Francis Busby, must stand out as fine examples to everyone and they were backed by a small army of people in Air Raid Precautions (later Civil Defence) who dealt with the nuts and bolts of the organisation of the County Borough's rescue and medical services as well as the wardens and many, many more — they are listed later.

Blood donors gladly offered blood to the local hospitals for use by civilian and service casualties; a casualty bureau dealt with all reports and queries about casualties before transmission to the Controller; the staff of the control room did a remarkable job co-ordinating the organisations reporting and dealing with incidents; the rescue services,

however, were the most respected — their devotion to duty, outstanding courage, speed, efficiency and skill were of the highest order and, when infinite patience and compassion were required when working in the most treacherous conditions, they produced those, too. They saw the dirtiest and bloodiest part of the war as it affected Eastbourne and the townspeople will be eternally grateful to them all.

The medical services — doctors, nurses and first aid parties, professionals or volunteers like the Red Cross and St John Ambulance Brigade — were also immensely brave and unstinting in their efforts to help the injured. The Air Raid Wardens had to know their localities and who lived where so that, in the event of an incident, they could suggest possible numbers of trapped people to be rescued. They fought fires, commenced rescue work, applied first aid and gave succour to the shocked or homeless — vital work

Another victim is hurried away from the scene of devastation by grim-faced rescuers from civilian and military organisations and bystanders.

which undoubtedly saved innumerable lives.

Despite the damage to its tracks, rolling stock and buildings, the Southern Railway Company and its employees provided a remarkable service to and from the town with only minimal disruptions to the timetables. A railway is a legitimate target for bombers but nobody flinched from duty.

Another legitimate target was the Eastbourne Gas Company's works beside Lottbridge Drove and gasholders there were hit a number of times but elsewhere in the town, scarcely a raid occurred without a gas main being fractured and, as often as not, taking fire. Even so, the number of times the gas was completely cut off to premises for any appreciable length of time was surprisingly small.

The Eastbourne Corporation Electricity Department also suffered damage to its mains and, to some extent, its buildings but in general managed to keep the generators running and, at a time of smaller demand from the town, to feed power into the national grid to help the rest of the country.

The oldest publicly-owned bus undertaking in the world — Eastbourne Corporation Motor Omnibus Department (the initials are immortalised in ECMOD Road) — suffered severe damage to its buildings and vehicles, had eight buses requisitioned by government agencies, hired out fifteen double-deckers to an operator in Lancashire, provided transport for workers on defence projects after Dunkirk and were on stand-by to move their buses inland to provide transport for army reserves in the event of invasion. At the worst point of the war, when the town's population shrank to its lowest figure, the bus undertaking showed a drop in passengers to one-seventh of the normal figure.

Southdown Motor Services also suffered losses and damage during the war and offered similar services to the authorities as those of the town bus undertaking.

Before the war, the Eastbourne Waterworks Company took steps to ensure the continuity of supply in the event of air attacks on the town, recruiting local plumbers as auxiliary turncocks in case of emergency. The town was divided into areas about half-a-mile wide and each area was provided with a standpipe so that every house in the town was within 500 yards of pure water in case of a complete breakdown of mains supplies, and all hospitals were equipped with their own storage tanks. Thanks to the skill and efficiency of the company staff, there was seldom any major disruption of supplies no matter the extent of damage to mains supplies.

A workman, repairing a Langney Road roof after an earlier raid, was injured in the leg during another attack. First to reach him was a first aid worker who climbed from a window and up onto the roof before the fire brigade could come to his assistance.

The Eastbourne detachment of the Royal Observer Corps pose in the Saffrons with the uniforms they only received late in the war. Without their sharp eyes and ears, many an incoming aircraft would have gone undetected and no warning given.

The Royal Observer Corps are the unsung heroes of the war in Eastbourne. These men had no uniforms until the third year of war and even then had to part with valuable clothing coupons before receiving them. They stuck to their posts through all weathers, using eyes and ears to supplement the radar stations' efforts and, often enough, being the first to report the approach of enemy aircraft, especially when they came in under the radar at sea level.

When at last a local warning system was approved by the Home Office, the Observers could notify the Controller of an incoming attack and he would then authorise the immediate sounding of the new warning. But even this still resulted in catastrophic delays and the Observers took matters into their own hands and had the sirens sounded on their own initiative. They were reprimanded for this 'high-handed' action but persisted and eventually won official permission to continue.

Although very often bombing cut off electricity and gas to the local Press, it was much to the credit of every man and woman on their staffs that never once was an edition missed. T.R. Beckett Ltd (then of Pevensey Road), the town's principal newspaper proprietors, published the Eastbourne Gazette and Herald, the Worthing Herald and the Shoreham Herald at that time. Eastbourne Chronicle Ltd, of South Street, produced its own paper and Strange the Printer, of Grove Road and York Road, produced the Eastbourne Courier — only the latter publication being printed on 'flat-bed' presses.

So, despite certain reporting restrictions, the townspeople could reckon on seeing the news as usual except that complete details and pictures of raids would often have to wait three weeks. Government edict declared that when a raid took place the next local editions could not refer directly to it having taken place in Eastbourne and so, the town became 'a south coast town', only becoming Eastbourne after a lapse of a few weeks. The idea was to deny the enemy detailed information of the effect of his attacks but was more a bureaucratic aberration than a useful ploy.

Finally, a word in defence of that much-maligned and mis-represented organisation, the Home

A posed scene in the ARP Control Room where all incidents were plotted and assistance co-ordinated.

Sergeant Charles Arnold of 10 Platoon, 'C' Company, 21st (Eastbourne) Battalion Sussex Home Guard, receives attention for a minor injury received while assisting in rescue work.

Guard. The men who volunteered to take their part in defending their country in the event of a German invasion were far from the 'company of fools' painted by the Press and, more recently, television. The majority had already fought the Germans in the bloodiest war in history and they viewed the rematch with the eyes of men saddened by the circumstances which forced them back into uniform — but they never flinched and they never bragged.

From its inception as 'G' Company of the Sussex Local Defence Volunteers in May 1940, the 21st (Eastbourne) Battalion, Sussex Home Guard, was equipped with service calibre rifles — not shotguns and not 'pikes' but proper rifles and ammunition. By the time the invasion was due, they were fully equipped with rifles, Browning automatic rifles, Tommy guns, Browning medium machine-guns and grenades.

Their brief was to 'observe, report and harass' the enemy at every turn and were only to stand and fight if 'cut off in close contact'.

At first designated a mere company, within a few days, the Eastbourne unit had grown larger than most army infantry battalions and was so designated. Guards were mounted at vulnerable points about the town and anti-parachutist patrols were established where the land contours provided a good view over suitable drop-zones. In Eastbourne's case, however, being cut off in close contact was inevitable as the town would have been outflanked early on in the invasion and there would have been no option but to

Lieutenant Freddie Morris and men of 10 Platoon, 'C' Company, 21st (Eastbourne) Battalion, Sussex Home Guard, await an umpire's order to commence an exercise.

stand and fight right from the outset.

Later, the danger lay in 'raids in force' against the coast, and the Home Guard was on alert for this eventuality at all times. Also, their weapon state improved to the point when they had what was designated 'sub-artillery', capable of stopping the toughest tanks then existing.

Forget 'Dad's Army', think of 2,000 Eastbourne men patiently waiting for an enemy who, despite his boasting, never accepted the risks attendant upon mounting an invasion.

The local battalion was commanded, variously, by: Brigadier-General E.W. Costello, VC, CMG, CVO, DSO; Colonel Wise, DSO; Brigadier Charles Terrott, DSO, and Lieutenant-Colonel T. Sutton, MBE, and altogether 5,000 men passed through the battalion as younger men were called-up into full-time service and fresh volunteers replaced them.

Eastbourne, that staid 'Empress of Watering Places' pre-war home of pride, pomposity and class consciousness, emerged as a town of united people who could hold up their heads secure in the knowledge that they had not been found wanting when courage, comradeship, cheerfulness and sheer tenacity of purpose were most demanded.

A crowd gathers outside Eastbourne Town Hall to hear the results of the first election to be held after the war.

Civil defence officials

ARP Controller: W.H. Smith (Chief Constable) (Retired April 1, 1943). Succeeded by: F.H. Busby (Town Clerk)

Deputy ARP Controllers: Mr J.A. Fairclough and Inspector R.S. Crighton.

Chief Warden: Brig-Gen. E.W. Costello, VC, CMG, CVO, DSO. Succeeded in November 1939 by: Sir George Lambert, KCSI.

Deputy Chief Warden: Sir Robert Dodd, CSI.

Chief Assistant: P/Sgt John Bull.

ARP Officer: Major G.H. Christie. Succeeded on August 1, 1940 by: Inspector R.S. Crighton.

Assistant ARP Officer: Mr H.J. Wood.

National Fire Service (formerly Eastbourne Fire Brigade and Auxiliary Fire Service): Chief Officer S.A. Phillips.

Police: Superintendent Archer (From April 1, 1943).

Senior Control Room Duty Officer: Mr H.J. Wood. Succeeded on January 1, 1944 by: Mr A.J. Page.

Responsible for Rescue Services: Mr R. Williams (Borough Surveyor).

Rescue Services Staff Officer: Mr R.V. Harvey.

Casualty, First Aid and Hospital Services: Dr J. Fenton (Medical Officer of Health).

Staff Officer to MOH: Mr H.T. Hounsom.

Assistant Staff Officer (responsible for training): Mr A.J. Burnage.

First Aid Commandant: Dr R.M. Barron.

Senior Gas Identification Officer: Mr L.P. Blackwell.

Gas Identification Officer: Coun. G. Bignell.

Assistant Gas Identification Officer: Mr S.J. Hounsom.

Food Decontamination Officer: Mr A. Lindfield.

Assistant Food Decontamination Officers: Mr G.N. Richards and Mr F.T. Rippin.

Transport Officer: Mr J. Atherton.

Women's Transport Service: Mrs E.M. Gurd (Commandant); Miss M.K. Slocombe (Deputy).

Billeting Officer: Mr R. Ticehurst.

Public Assistance and Relieving Officer (for persons made homeless by enemy action): Mr R.S. Pickover.

Superintendent Mortuary Service: Mr R. Hall.

Police Mortuary Service: P/Sgt Kenward and PC Goldsmith.

Communications Officer: Mr H.J. Wood.

Royal Observer Corps: C/O J.E.F. May (Head Observer). Succeeded in 1942 by: C/O C.E. Lawrence. Deputy: L/O N.W. Hardy.

Fire Guard Officer: P/Sgt E. Weaver. Succeeded in 1942 by: Superintendent A. Stevens.

Where the bombs hit Eastbourne

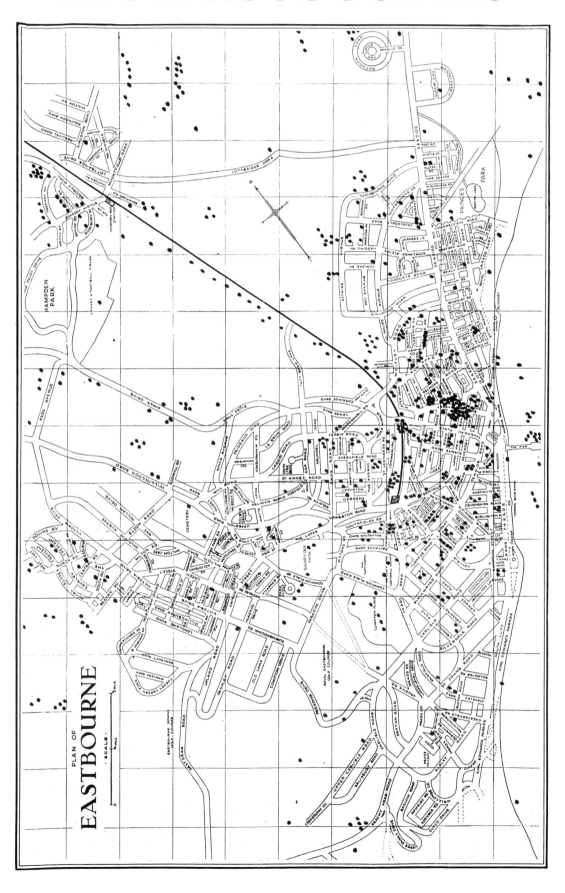

Flying Bombs —
the crash sites

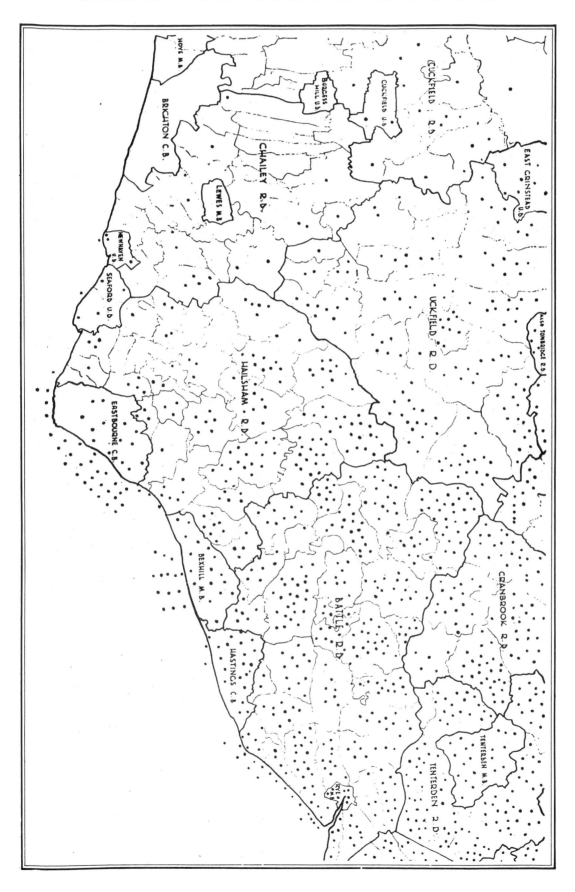

Roll of honour

DEATHS DUE TO ENEMY ACTION

(Local residents only: public, ARP/Civil Defence, Police, Fire Brigade, etc.)

ANKER, Mrs Edith M.
ARNOLD, Mrs Lily
ASHDOWN, Mrs Cecily Amy
BAILEY, Mr J.W.
BAGSHAWE, Miss Amy
BAKER, Grayson Wynne
BAKER, Mrs Mary Ann
BATES, Francis
BENJAMIN, Claude R.
BLAKE, Cecil W.
BONFIGLIOLI, Christopher
BONFIGLIOLI, Mrs Dorothy
BONIFACE, Mrs Ethel May
BONIFACE, Mortimer
BONIFACE, William
BONNER, Miss Anna
BONTOFT, John Harrison
BOUCHER, Miss S.
BOWEN, Mrs Marjorie F.
BRADFORD, Sydney
BRITTAIN, Henry Edward
BROOK, Miss Mary
BURGESS, Charles
BURTENSHAW, Louise R. (15)
CHAMBERS, Mrs Beatrice H.M.
CHAPMAN, Mrs E.
CHAPMAN, Wilfred John
CHATFIELD, Mrs Ruth
CHENNELL, Mr Eric
CHERRYMAN, Mrs Eleanor F.
CHILD, Miss Annie
CHITTY, Pearl May
COCKBURN, Mrs Jessie M.
COLLIER, Alfred
COLVIN, Mrs Annie
COOPER, Mrs A.M.
CREE, Mrs Ruth
CRISP, Mrs Mary A.
CROMWELL, William A.
CROWHURST, Mrs Frances E.
CROWHURST, Miss Louisa Emily
CURRIE, Miss Auguston
DANN, Mrs Lucy
DAVIES, Mrs Kathleen
DE LA ROCHE, Cornelius
DOBELL, Mrs Alice K.
DORMAN, George O.
DRY, Mrs Charlotte Elizabeth
DUKE, Frederick Roy
EDMONDS, Mr W.J.
EDWARDS, Frank Bertram
ELLETT, Anthony (5)
ELSON, Mrs Ethel
FLY, Brian (6)
FREEMAN, William

GEARING, Mrs Rose F.
GILES, Mrs Olive G.
GILES, Stanley Arthur
GILLIES, David
GLEN, William H.
GOACHER, Walter H.
GOSDEN, Mr F.
GOWER, Douglas (13)
GRAHAM, Mrs M.A.
GRANT, F.M.
GRANT, Mrs Mary P.
GRIFFIN, John E.
GURR, Mrs Daisy Ruth
GURR, Thomas H.
GUY, Mrs A.
HALL, Lucy
HARDWICK, Miss Doris K.
HARLAND, Peggy (17)
HARRIES, Mrs J.E.
HART, Mrs Ethel L.
HENMAN, Samuel
HILLIDGE, Benjamin
HIPGRAVE, Miss I.
HIPWELL, Miss Violet A.
HOLLEBON, Miss Alice
HOLLEBON, Miss Annie
HOLLEBON, Miss Henrietta
HORTON, Peter (12)
HUDSON, Mrs Laura O.
HUGHES, Mrs Matilda
HUNTER, John Edward
HURD, Frank
HUTCHINSON, Joseph
HUTCHINSON, Sydney Alfred
HYLANDS, Mrs Lily Norma
JACKSON, Lily
JENSEN, Hans
JONES, Miss Ann L.
KEAY, Ethelbert Norman
KELLY, Mr A.J.
LANGFORD, Charles J.
LAWRENCE, Miss Rose
LAWRY, Miss Carol Winifred
LEITCH, Mr A.
LONGWORTH, Mr H.L.
MACKAY, Donald G.
McKINLEY, Mrs Edith.
MARCHANT, Mrs Harriett
MARLEY, Samuel
MASON, Ernest E.
MATTHEWS, Mrs Winifred M.
MEWETT, Frederick George
MOORE, Frank
NEWMAN, Albert Edward
NICHOLLS, Mrs Eva F.

NICHOLLS, Michael (9 months)
NORMAN, Miss Florence E.
OLIVER, Miss A.K.
OWENS, Dennis John
PACKHAM, Mrs Emily Elizabeth
PAYNE, Mr J.
PAYTON, Mrs E.
PAYTON, William J.
PENFOLD, Mary Adeline (16)
PERRY, Miss Margaret
PERRY, Miss Mary
PIDCOCK, Arthur
PINNINGTON, Harry
PINNINGTON, Mrs E.
PRINGLE, Miss Anne Elizabeth
PRINGLE, Miss Christine Jane
PRINGLE, Miss Emily Gertrude
PRIOR, Mrs Grace E.
PRODGER, Miss F.L.
RANDALL, Mrs Emily Julia
RAYNER, Mrs Daisy M.
RAYNER, Joseph
RICH, Charles
RICHARDSON, Mrs Mary M.
RIPLEY, David Ronald (14)
RIPLEY, Mrs Mabel
RIPLEY, Moses
RIPLEY, William
SARGENT, George O.
SAYERS, Rose
SCOTT, Mrs Edith
SELWAY, Mrs Florrie Myra
SHADBOLT, Harry
SHERWOOD, Mrs Beatrice Maud
SHERWOOD, Joan (10)

SHERWOOD, Keith Arthur (5)
SIMMONDS, Mrs Emily Louisa
SMITH, Mrs Ellen
SMITH, Mr J.P.
SOUTHGATE, Mr D.R.Y.
STANDEN, Frederick
STEED, Mr J.
STEVENS, John
STEVENS, Thomas E.
STRONG, Mrs Lottie M.
TAYLOR, Mrs Mary Moira
TAYLERSON, Miss Emily
THORNE, G.
THORNE, Mrs L.G.
TIDEY, Mrs Sarah
TURNER, Jean (11)
TURNER, William Thomas
TYDEMAN, Miss Ellen J.
VAN MULBREGT, Jacobus
VAN MULBREGT, Mrs F.W.
VIGOR, Jane Emily
VINSEN, Theobald
WALKER, Betty
WALKER, Mrs W.E.
WALTERS, Mrs Mary Ann
WHITE, Mrs Eliza Mary Ann
WHITE, Henry Frederick
WILKINS, Mrs E.L.
WILKINSON, Mrs Myrtle Olive
WILLIAMS, Mrs Ellen
WILLSON, Miss Kate Louisa
WILSON, Miss Evelyn Margaret
WISE, Mrs Henrietta
WOOLLIAMS, Robert
WREN, Mrs Fanny

At last! Anti-tank and anti-landing mines have been cleared
from a limited area of beach and children can run down to the
sea and sands they have been able only to see, hear and smell
for nearly four-and-a-half years. The scaffold pole obstacles
erected to hinder the landing of vehicles offer little hindrance
to the children as they eagerly scramble through.